The Death of Rabelais

The Death of Rabelais

A PLAY

by

J. C. Scharl

WITH A FOREWORD BY TARA ISABELLA BURTON

Wiseblood Books

Copyright © 2025 Wiseblood Books, J. C. Scharl

WISEBLOOD BOOKS
Joshua Hren, Editor-in-Chief
Post Office Box 870
Menomonee Falls, WI 53052
www.wisebloodbooks.com

Cover art: The Ant and the Grasshopper by Jehan Georges Vibert
https://www.artic.edu/artworks/29730/the-ant-and-the-grasshopper

ISBN: 978-1-951319-20-5

For my children

Contents

Foreword	i
Dramatis Personae	vii
Act I	9
Act II	53
Act III	105
Acknowledgements	165
About J. C. Scharl	167
About Tara Isabella Burton	169

For the LORD will pass through to strike the Egyptians; but when He sees the blood on the lintel and on the two doorposts, the LORD will pass over the door and will not allow the destroyer to come into your houses to strike you.
Exodus 12:23

But we do see Him who was made for a little while lower than the angels, namely, Jesus, because of His suffering death crowned with glory and honor, so that by the grace of God He might taste death for everyone.
Hebrews 2:9

Foreword

Tara Isabella Burton

I had the pleasure of experiencing the first installment of Jane Clark Scharl's *Rabelais* trilogy, the existential murder mystery *Sonnez Les Matines,* in what was perhaps its ideal setting. About a year ago, a few friends and I—members of a New York City theatre club with a black box theatre space—produced a staged reading of the play. Over a few rehearsals, and on the day of the production itself, we brought to dramatic life not only Scharl's vivid, highly theatrical characters but also her continually delightful and surprising verse.

On the page, Scharl's gift for poetry is already apparent in the delight she takes in the capacity of language to upend, to complicate, to draw connections unexpected and revelatory. In Scharl's verse, language is not a vehicle of divine creation *ex nihilo*—words that make something out of nothing—but rather a deeply, messily human attempt to see the links, the meaning, *between* elements of a confusing creation that, to us mortals, at least, oftentimes seems absurd. Language, for Scharl, lies between body and soul, between the sounds of our throats and the shapes of the angels; it is not a refuge from flesh but rather a constant, as it were, dialogue with it.

Out loud, in the bodies and voices and faces of actors, the erotic materialism of Scharl's language is all the more evident. And nowhere is it more evident than in the bawdy, bombastic person of François Rabelais—doctor, priest, scholar, and satirist—and the through-line of Scharl's eventual trilogy. "Love Wisdom," Rabelais urges us, in *Sonnez Les Matines'* closing speech, "but not with what's above! / She's a pretty girl, and ripe; love her / with your body, your skin and bones, the gurgle / of your gut; love her with your rutting heart."

Rabelais is *Sonnez Les Matines'* most compelling character—and, one suspects, the figure whose approach to language most closely matches

Scharl's own. So it is a particular treat to meet him again in *The Death of Rabelais*: a play not only as riotously carnivalesque as its predecessor, but even more explicit—and moving—in its exploration of what the carnivalesque might mean, in the light of both Ordinary Time and Lent.

Rabelais is no hedonist, at least not as a modern, secular audience might understand the term. His interest in sex is not prurient, but rather—to use a word oft-misused—"life-affirming." In his time, Rabelais may have been considered a controversial figure by Catholic and Protestant alike, but Scharl reveals to us a fundamental orthodoxy in Rabelais's seeming transgression. Rabelais's interest in "fur, flesh and faeces" is also a commitment to what the Catholic poet Gerald Manley Hopkins has called *inscape*: the fundamental, embodied *thisness* of a being. Rabelais writes about, speaks about, poeticizes all those elements of our existence that we find too uncomfortable to call to mind. But, in doing so, he helps us sanctify them.

In *Sonnez Les Matines*, Rabelais infuriates his interlocutors—an arrogant young Ignatius of Loyola and a dyspeptic John Calvin—with his irreverent humanism, but in *The Death of Rabelais*, we see a more mature, if hardly more "grown-up," Rabelais, and feel the full theological weight of his convictions. The inherent meaningfulness of this embodied world, he suggests, makes sense only against a backdrop in which God became man; the fact of the Incarnation seems, to Rabelais, to in turn demand a love for Wisdom as "rutting" as it is sincere. The Rabelaisian stance, rather than one philosophical option among three, becomes instead in *The Death of Rabelais* at once an internally cohesive and gloriously polyphonic invitation to fall in love with humanity—warts, farts, and all.

The Death of Rabelais is a brilliant, beautiful, bawdy play. It is also *tragi-comic*, a word that is often overused to mean both funny and sad at the same time, but in this instance evokes Scharl's ability—especially through the eyes of Rabelais—to see humor's power as a mechanism for both transgression and, through the strangeness of that transgression, love. For Rabelais, humor—and its power to poke holes in our own self-certainty—does not just destabilize our conceptions of our own selves and of others and of society, but also, all the more importantly, destabilizes our disposition towards despair. When we laugh at Death, or with her, we recognize that the tragedy of her inevitability is not all there is. Or, as Rabelais's foil, the Friar, puts it with a little more flair:

> Humor's a relief! It shows the truth.
> Every laugh's a window on the void—
> crack jokes with me, and by them crack the world's
> facade to show the bedlam underneath!

Yet that Bedlam, for Rabelais, is a creative rather than a destructive force. In punning style, he goes on to convince us that:

> Humor is no chaos, but the very
> drip and flow of everything, the sticky
> fluid carrying life up from stodgy
> soil to all these many moistening bodies . . .
> humor is our unity, our scope,
> our element, our one and only hope
> to make disjointed things one whole; to weave
> from severed threads a spread 'neath which to cleave
> and there conceive, with giggles and with wiggles,
> an unimagined jest; to nimbly wriggle
> past the facts of life to breathe its farts
> and still to hug it close—now that is art!

The bones, as it were, of *The Death of Rabelais* are tragic. Violette loves Alain, who loves Martine—as does Violette's hapless brother Robert. Martine still pines, we learn, for Renaud: a friar who has left her for holy orders. And yet, in Scharl's telling, and through Rabelais's eyes, it is in moments of comedy—be they the slightly farcical play the characters perform in Act II, or less bombastic interchanges between the characters, as when Violette scandalizes the men at table with a dirty-seeming riddle that turns out to have an innocuous answer—that the mess of these characters' humanity becomes most apparent. Their hearts, as ill-governed as their bodies, plunge them all into an emotional maelstrom in which, somehow, God makes His presence felt.

This is the note Scharl keeps striking—each time with more intensity.

Our bodies, our desires, our *human* confusion over love lost or won or consummated, our sacrifices, are not impediments to God's grace but rather the site of God's transformation. Yes, sin keeps us from God, but it is also the wound God touches to heal us. Violette tells us, convincingly, that "Our flesh is laced too tightly; we can't rip it off to ease our swollen souls, alas"; but the theology that runs through *Death of Rabelais* is always an incarnational one: in which the enfleshment of our souls is constitutive of their reality.

In one of the play's most moving—and theologically rich passages—Scharl makes this argument even more clearly. During an Epiphany masque, the Friar Renaud, portraying the Devil, claims superiority to God and man alike as the firstborn creation that outstrips the Creator. Thus does the Devil accuse God of envy of His own:

> the splendid blend of power and perception
> that I am, for you had learned at last
> what man has yet to learn: the thing made,
> if made greatly, will outpace the maker.
> The father always marvels at his son's
> achievements. But your arts must not outrun you;
> you must hobble them, bind them to bodies
> and to birthing and to pain, and if
> all else fails, if through magnificence
> they defy your limitations, rise
> to something great, you fling them down.

Our weak bodies, for the Devil, are evidence of God's fear of what man, untrammeled, might be. And yet Wisdom replies: "there is a Son already." We may be bound to bodies, but so too has God bound Himself: to pain, to flesh, and—at last—to death.

Here, Death is not merely a corpse or a construct but a character in her own right, occasioning a night of revelations between lovers past and present, on the fascinated outside of human frailty. We learn little of who Death is, or what she wants—except that Rabelais, and all the merrymakers of the festal night, intrigue her. She is not bound to humanity; nevertheless, access to it changes her. Her experience of human desire, and moreover, human *humor*—the dissonance of the unexpected; the surprise reversal—has done to her what the shock of death does so often to us. And it reminds us that Death, literally or figuratively, doesn't have the final word.

Or, as Rabelais muses, after the mysterious events of Epiphany's Eve have played out:

> And yet upon this night Death laughed. Forget
> everything in life but that: Death
> upon Epiphany, found mirth. The depth
> of that's unknown, the import, and the scope—
> but maybe after all there's room for hope
> that as Christ, the Laughter of the Father,
> took laughter down to death, he made them brothers,
> and raising one, he equal raised the other,
> so even as he bears to God the marks
> of death, he leaves in death the very sparks
> of merriment!

It is a shame that not all readers of this marvelous play—at once deeply serious and deeply *funny*—will have the opportunity, as I did with *Sonnez Les Matines*, to hear it performed (although I certainly encourage anyone reading this to get a group of friends together some wintry night and do just that). But even on the page, *The Death of Rabelais* helps us to better understand the wriggling contradictions of embodiment—and to see, in its paradox, the mystery of the Incarnation. And it helps us understand, too, why comedy—earthly and divine—might be the most fitting genre in which to tell that story.

DRAMATIS PERSONAE
(in order of appearance and including whom they play within the Play in Act II)

François RABELAIS,
a monk and writer who thinks himself midway along the journey of his life. He trades his Jester's cap for a black robe, and plays Providence.

DEATH,
a laborer who has come to take a soul. She trades her black robe for a Jester's cap, and plays Wisdom.

FRIAR RENAUD,
a friar who claims to have many friends. He wears no costume but his own self, and plays the Devil.

MICHEL LAVIGNE,
a wine merchant who has despaired even of drink. He wears a Pilgrim's costume, and plays a Minor Fiend.

ALAIN COURCETTE,
a young man who is engaged and eager, perhaps overly so, to be married. He wears a King's costume, and plays the Man.

VIOLETTE PRUD'HOMME,
a clever girl who will have what she wants. She wears a Priest's costume, and plays the Sun.

ROBERT PRUD'HOMME,
a man who is willing to be ashamed. He wears a Mother's costume, and plays Father (and Tree).

MARTINE BARRE
a young woman who is engaged, but reluctant, to be married. She wears a Queen's costume, and plays the Lady.

ACT I

*Scene I: A dark night—January 5*th*, the eve of Epiphany, the region of Champagne. The road runs through desolate wintry vineyards, and a freak snowstorm has blown up. A strong wind is in evidence. Across this scene tramps RABELAIS, a small pack on his back, walking with obvious difficulty. He is wearing a tattered and garish cape of several colors in broad patches, and a cap that has been ingeniously split into two peaks, each tipped in tiny clay bells, though the effort is clearly slapdash. The road is deserted, but forks at the center of the stage. There is no road sign. Reaching this crossroad, RABELAIS stops.*

RABELAIS

Now what is this? No crossroad should be here.

(He draws his cloak around himself against the wailing wind and blowing snow. Throughout the following speech he stamps his feet, rubs his hands, and demonstrates increasing dismay.)

    This road should run straight through the yards, and clear
    on to my aim, but now behold: my one
    road has become two, even worse than none.
    My brain's not equal to the choice; tell me,
    someone, where to go, since I'm not free
    to follow in some simple way! Wicked
    days—each fool must walk the road he's picked.
    Though what road I've picked, I cannot say—
    hanging between patrons, every day
    accusèd by some former friend of what

I yesterday denounced, all tiny cuts
but chisels to my soul, till I don't know
myself if I am heretic or hero,
conspirator or clown, prophet or
pariah . . . and all because I write a more
cheerful tale than my fellows do!
The world's reforming, sure, and to a rougher
mold. All lines are sharper, chuckles gruffer,
slighter margin now for mirth, and every
joke's a body only fit to bury.
I start to doubt if comedy is true,
or if the surface only of this world
is joy, and in the depths lies sorrow curled.

(*Thunder cracks and lightning flashes; it is that rare combination of a blizzard and a thunderstorm. RABELAIS looks around for shelter, but there is none.*)

How this wind blows! *Blows*, now there's a word at once
a thing and not a thing . . . there never was a dunce
took heavier blows from iron fist than I from empty
wind today! What are these awful puns? Folly,
help me! My humor's stopped and soured! This must be
  Death.
And on Epiphany Eve! When I sprawl, out of breath,
upon this chilly Earth, I've an epiphany
forthcoming—*the* epiphany, most probably,
the last epiphany, the world's buttocks fleeing
as I freeze . . . that's for me, if I don't quickly
escape this wind!
                This is when philosophers

would rattle on about existence, and adjure
me to accept the evil fate I'm given, indenture
myself to death's teeth upon my throat, secure
his cape while I am strangled by it, capitulate
my head to every swinging axe, situate
my grave here in this humdrum place, consider
the stars whirling above my space and not be bitter.
Oh no! along with many other Latinate
words that play so nicely underneath the sedate
Tuscan sun but here, what here? Who bids me revel
in this outrageous weather? Who besides the Devil
has the fiery balls to mention, as my nose
and fingers freeze, how sweetly, freely my soul goes!
Who, in a maelstrom, bandies possibility
with airy spirits hellbent on hostility?

(As he speaks, from up the road behind him comes DEATH, played by a slight young woman with a shaved head, wrapped in a black cloak and carrying a miniature organ or pipes. She is clearly dressed as a traditional DEATH character, but the effect is muted. The FRIAR is close behind, but not yet visible to RABELAIS. The scene must be blocked so that RABELAIS thinks DEATH is with the FRIAR, and the FRIAR thinks DEATH is with RABELAIS.)

DEATH
(with a strangely child-like earnestness)

Well, you, apparently.

RABELAIS

(startled)
Who's this? Fellow traveler or sprite,
if you know this road, please put me right
before I'm lost between the dark and light!
Do you know the road to Nancy?

DEATH

(regretfully, with the same strangely serious but innocent tone)
I do, but I do not think you will.

RABELAIS

(He is slightly baffled; he is looking for repartee and is confused to find this straightforwardness. He retorts.)
Ah, neither quick nor kind—what kind of answer's
that? And more, what kind of man would make
that kind? Answer: one who isn't quick.

(DEATH smiles, and RABELAIS looks more closely.)
Or one who isn't a man? Good maid, what brings
you out upon a night like this alone?
It's neither safe nor wise, but I admire
you for it, and will aid you if I can!

DEATH

(looking behind down the road to where the FRIAR will appear)
It's long since any mortal man tendered
aid to *me*, instead what I've wrought.

(*RABELAIS is clearly confused by this statement, but before he can reply there is another lightning flash. FRIAR RENARD comes huffing up out of the storm. He stops when he sees the two, then lets out a shout and approaches RABELAIS, clapping him on the back and drawing him into a stout embrace. RABELAIS's greeting is equally enthusiastic.*)

FRIAR

François! You filthy rogue! Vision as priceless
in these wastelands as a pretty whore,
rare as docile wife, scarce as virgin
lady, exotique as sated spinster!
What brings you to this sightless road upon
Epiphany? I thought you in Paris! (*Holds him at arms' length
    and beams at him.*)

RABELAIS

Well, you know, things change—like the weather,
how things change! Paris is an ever-
crueler nest for little fledglings . . . one was
burned not long ago, and because
intriguement with the process seems to spread
and because of some witty things I've said—
such funny things! Scholarly jokes and such—
well, Paris became a little much.
But enough! I'd wish us together
by a cheerful fire for this, rather
than tossed about out here like cast-off feathers.
Tell me, brother, do you know which way

to Nancy? I must be there by day. *(Under his breath and
glancing at DEATH)*
Though I'd give much to find what brings you here
abroad at night beside this strange familiar!

FRIAR

Nancy! A very Fool you are indeed—
you'll not get there tonight. It is five hours
walk in goodly air, but on this night
of snow and fire, all powers on the hunt,
the Devil himself would hardly dare to try it,
though if that is the way you're set, I'd chance
it for a chance to prance with you. *(Aside, so RABELAIS
cannot hear.)*
As well as penetrate the pretty puzzle
of this pert companion you have with you . . .
Not quite the proper thing for wandering monks! *(He chuckles
crudely to himself.)*

RABELAIS

I am convinced. That's not our way.

FRIAR
(looking at DEATH with curiosity, but addressing RABELAIS)

Take heart! I've better plans for you than death
among the vines. What say you to this?
Not half an hour's walk away, we'll find
a country house, the house where I was raised,

for all intents, and there, we will find,
gathered in festive mirth such maidens as one
thirsts to see, such wines as quench that thirst,
and naughty games to stir not only heart
in chest but blood in flesh! Who does not long
in these so frigid days to see a smile
and clasp a hand—or more—in true fondness?
Come with me! There's room for all and more!
They are as my kin; you'll be my guests,
and gladly they'll convert you into friends.

(ALL three turn and continue down the road. Lightning cracks again. They walk through the speeches that follow.)

RABELAIS

If it's a feast we're bound to join,
I fear we have but scanty coin
to change . . . we have only these costumes
which we know are the only custom
acccpted at these fêtes, but lo,
behold, how paltry is our show!
A tattered cape or two! It's true,
your habit's got its faults, but you
will patch up all its holes, I'm sure,
through long-held love. But we! Allure
we've none; no glamour to these robes,
no spangled masks nor fiery globes
to dangle from our coats; no jeweled
cheeks, no flaming blade, no scaled

legs or double mouth, no blanched
leather, no gilded limbs and branched
wings, no fangs, halos, snouts,
nothing to offer these devout
roisterers but our selves—a comic
gift indeed!—our anatomic
persons unenhanced by stagecraft
or playacting . . . my friend, they'll laugh
at us, and no man dares invoke
such laughter as we will provoke!

DEATH

(gently intervening with genuine interest)

But there I think you're wrong;
I know No Man,
and he'd be muchly pleased.

FRIAR

(with nasty humor)

"I know no man!" Now that's a claim's been made
by many a maid and made as many a maid
a bride! But you've misread your scene a bit,
my girl—save your protests till they're asked for!
From two such shoddy celibates as this
you can expect nothing, or nothing decent! *(He makes a lewd
face or gesture.)*

RABELAIS
(curiously vexed)

For shame, Renaud, for shame! That isn't wit!
Does some vow drive you to submit
to such sardonic sleights as humor? Jeering
jibes are simple; any man can, sneering,
smear this goodly world God's made, and use
his holy gift of words to do so! But true
comedy—now that too few can do!

FRIAR
(backing down slightly)

Come, come, it's just a little jibe—
what after all's a joke besides a slip,
a broken thread, discontinuity
in what we want to think a rigid pattern?
Humor's a relief! It shows the truth.
Every laugh's a window on the void—
crack jokes with me, and by them crack the world's
facade to show the bedlam underneath!

RABELAIS
(irate)

What blasphemy is this? Infernal wicked-
ness, flatulence of hell, frigid
excrescent of the pit, putrescent fruit
of Devil's loins, swollen stinking root
of Satan's rotted tooth, canker-sore

hot on every demon's butt-cheek—more
noxious names I could produce but for
the presence of this maid, yet shame! Shame!
Unhappy fault that sunders now the name
of *humor* from its wholeness, from its aim.
On this I've staked my life, my reputation—
maybe my soul, without some dispensation
of fresh grace from Rome—this is my creed,
this is what I believe, my word and deed.
Humor is no chaos, but the very
drip and flow of everything, the sticky
fluid carrying life up from stodgy
soil to all these many moistening bodies . . .
humor is our unity, our scope,
our element, our one and only hope
to make disjointed things one whole; to weave
from severed threads a spread 'neath which to cleave
and there conceive, with giggles and with wiggles,
an unimagined jest; to nimbly wriggle
past the facts of life to breathe its farts
and still to hug it close—now that is art!
Noblest science, in which the trampled heart
makes the mud its marriage bed; bright dart
to pierce the mind's armor... this is not
mere irony or mocking jabs, oh no!
Comedy is farce! a wink, a snort,
a chortle and a kick somewhere below,
a slap, a sigh, a grin and wonder why

one's pants are wet when the Earth and sky
alike are dry; a frisk, a flourish, a snap
and shout, the crack of towel against bare ass;
a high tide of verbiage in the mouth,
a glut of roughage in the sewage trough;
pleasure, precision, perception all become—
however bleak—by humor, chucklesome,
and in becoming so, become all one.

FRIAR
(laughs, irritating RABELAIS)

My wit may be more dry, but still, it rattles
less than yours in bitter winds like these.

DEATH
(unexpectedly, addressing the FRIAR)

Better living jokes that stink to Heaven
than drained ones moldering to stenchless dust.

FRIAR

Oh, so Death now gives opinions
about Humor! I'd have thought
your realms too far apart for that.

DEATH

The very distance gives me sight.

FRIAR

Do you know, this strange persuasion lends
to me a quite uncanny notion . . . Death
and Humor, abroad at one this reckless night!
This Death, though fresh, is not a merry consort.
Here's the thing, my girl *(turning to DEATH)*, you're
   overdone—
the drooping neck, the sagging bags,
the strippéd head, the hollow eyes,
the pale lips, it all adheres
too closely to the figure! There's no zest,
no carnivalesque sport to it, no jest!

RABELAIS
(to DEATH, kindly)

It's true; as Death you're in the range
of trite.

FRIAR

A rare Fool you'd make—a finer
fool most folk have never dreamed, a minor
miracle: a truly solemn Fool!

RABELAIS

Ah, now I see your prankish scheme! Look:
this severe mien joined not to sober Doom,
but Riot! How if this barren head did bloom
a jester's cap, and this determined tread

did sing with little bells, but all in deadly
earnest! No capers, tricks, not the unburnished
irony of a clown's thick-painted grin . . .
just gravity, pure as the Jovian tin,
and what's a better jest than that? Come,
good Death, switch robes with me! Become
the jester for some feast, so fearful grave,
you'll make all, with laughing, into slaves!

DEATH

I am already bound to feast—my own
strange feast, the one I'm always eating
and always shall be, till the end of days.
I come to bear away a soul.

FRIAR
(aside to RABELAIS)

            Clearly
she's mad—the gentlest and most playful thing's
to tolerate, even indulge her! *(To DEATH)* Kind
of you to come yourself! How singular
this soul must be to merit such attention.

DEATH
(mildly)

Perhaps; I only do as I am bid.

RABELAIS
(intervening)

We must get safely away from the wicked
wind, lest Death itself be whirled away
untimely and we be doomed to munch and crunch
the last forbidden fruit and be full damned!
We see what fearful remedy God wrought
to save us from eternal death—what would
it take to save us from eternal life?
Come, sweet maid! Embrace the feast, with all
its sports. Become our queen! Change robes with me!
It would be perfect comedy.

(DEATH considers, then replies.)
DEATH

It seems a harmless way to pass the night
before I claim the soul I'm sent to take.

RABELAIS
(hurriedly stripping off his robe and hat and handing them to DEATH)

There! That's it. Do nothing else—do just
that, you sprite. A fatal final end,
but of laughter! Here your cloak for mine,
ugh, that wind! It gets me to the bone.

FRIAR
(pulling off DEATH's robe)

Your hood's so fine, mam'selle!
No fear, you'll have it back tonight!
(To RABELAIS, but with an eye on DEATH)
A freakish kind of girl! What say
we strip her down a little far,
eh? And find out if the rest
of her's as bald as is that head!

(RABELAIS shoves the FRIAR away in disgust.)

FRIAR
(laughing)

That proves it! All those naughty words you write
are naught but words and the great Rabelais
is but a mincing spinster! I always knew!

RABELAIS

I write what I must write—every kind
of speech both pure and bawdy—all for joy,
man, for joy! If once my language harms
a gentle soul like this, stuff me forever
in a bag and tie it up and kick it!

DEATH
(interceding and speaking to RABELAIS)

I'll change with you, and beg you keep your lightsome
spirit, and miss no frolic for my sake.

FRIAR

See there, a sporting lass! And now, your pipes . . .
(He tries to take the pipes from DEATH, who grasps after them.)

DEATH

No, those I keep!

FRIAR

(holding the instrument aloft as DEATH clutches just the edge)
                Oh come
he won't break them, and what's a Death without
a tune? How shall he keep his time macabre?

(DEATH surrenders the pipes, and the FRIAR hands them to RABELAIS triumphantly. RABELAIS turns back to DEATH to adjust the costume.)

RABELAIS

Now, my cap . . . not back like that. Wear it
just so . . . well, you're no Triboulet, but that
may be for the best. His antics brought him
nose to nose with death a time too often!
Now, I contrive and . . . so!

(He spreads his arms as if presenting himself to a company.)
    Will it do?

(By the end of this speech, DEATH is draped in RABELAIS's parti-colored robe and wears his Jester's cap. RABELAIS is wearing DEATH's black robe [it's a little short on him, so he looks ridiculous] and carrying the pipes.)

DEATH

Will it do what?

RABELAIS
(with a huff of frustration)

Will it
do, will it do, will it pass
muster, will it fly, will it go,
will it cut it, come up to scratch, fit
the bill, cut the mustard? Will it wash,
will it carry water, will it hold up,
will it suffice? Will it measure water,
scratch a fly, hold the bill, muster
to fit, pass the mustard, cut the cheese?

DEATH

I cannot say. I'm only Death.

RABELAIS

No no, *I* am Death, and I intend to laugh
enough to make the grave sit up and dance!

DEATH
(a little sadly)

And since I am made Comedy, I must
drag laughter down into the grave with me.

FRIAR
(speaking with difficulty from laughing)

No better pair could I have conjured
from my own imaginings. You two
are proof that God runs just as far
ahead of us in comedy
as in any other virtue.

RABELAIS

If comedy's a virtue now,
then at last I've found my path
to Paradise and Heaven's feast!

DEATH

That path runs through a dreadful place
where this ill night would seem a summer's eve.

RABELAIS
*(his spirits rising with each line, he cuts capers
and frolics during this speech)*

Ah, but I prefer a winter feast!
In summer festivals, the ripened sweetness
is too keen. A simpering virgin bride
can't be arch because she knows no secrets.
A festival in winter, though . . . now *that's*
a lady I can love! A cunning widow
who trails me meekly down the aisle while
my buttocks tingle from her expert pinch!

(Turning to DEATH) You bid me keep my humor—this is it!
Good festival demands a smack, a little
tickle, a dark setting, some opposition.
A planet's clearest seen in retrograde
and not at home! Which is where you've been,
I guess, not to have seen the splendid revels
made to reveal the dancing bones of this,
our too too heavy age that, left unspanked,
would only sit and think on its demise.
But look! I am again the Fool! For that
is what we three are doing now, instead
of hying to whatever feast we find.

FRIAR

He's right! It's time we flee to that abode!
Spank me, Death, and set me on the road!

(DEATH does not oblige, so RABELAIS slaps the FRIAR on the rear and the two run offstage, cackling and slapping at each other, followed at a distance by DEATH.)

Scene II: RABELAIS, the FRIAR, and DEATH approach a house. Inside, the kitchen interior of a burgher home: broad slanted beams are visible overhead, and a fire roars in the fireplace. The lights are down; those inside are freezing. The room itself is richly decorated but uncomfortable. No one appears to be at ease. MARTINE and ALAIN sit at a table; he is drinking, she is not. ALAIN's king's crown is firmly on his head, while her queen's crown sits on the bar in front of her. LAVIGNE sits across from them holding a top that he appears to be spinning, his broad pilgrim's hat beside him on the bar. He wears a scallop-shell badge on his brown pilgrim's cloak. ROBERT, looking absurd in an ill-fitting costume of a heavily pregnant woman, sits a little way away beside VIOLETTE, who has loosened the belt on her priest costume.

(The three approach, then pause outside. As the FRIAR introduces the characters, either a light falls on them in turn or the one spoken of moves—something to indicate who is who. The FRIAR's tone indicates his relation to each member: LAVIGNE he introduces with a smile and warmth, ALAIN with a slighting tone, VIOLETTE indulgently, ROBERT dismissively, MARTINE with reserve and some bitterness. Even as he insults them, he clearly has affection for them all—the unchanging kind that comes of long acquaintance.)

FRIAR

See, there's the house, and those within my heart's
own friends, my kin, as dear to me as sun
and rain to saplings in the copse. There's

Lavigne, a very devil, whose father
merchants wine from Alsace to the Loire
and on feast days pours gratis drink for all—
his son's as dry as he is sweet, and stings.
The King you see, whose head's too small to wear
the crown, that's young Alain, whose father peddles
cinnamon and musk from the far East.
One clove's worth more than Alain's good opinion.
The girl cavorting as a priest is raffish
Violette, a wit who's always pregnant
with some secret scheme; don't offend her.
All things she'll forget but none forgive.
Robert's her brother, looking less absurd
than usual . . . a pigeon, meal-fed
and in-cream-stewed, a butter-faced fool!

RABELAIS

A merry crew you've brought us to.

FRIAR

I love them all, as truly as my heart
loves its own blood. *(A pause.)*

DEATH
(breaking in gravely)
                What of the other?

FRIAR

(for the first time showing something less than absolute confidence)
That is Martine.
This is her home, where truly she is Queen.
(Before RABELAIS can interrupt, he continues.)
These are my all, my dear ones. They know nothing
of my coming; this journey was scarce planned,
and little do they think to see me now.
So! Let's plan a game with them; in fun
alarm them with our unknown company
and brine the sweetness of this night with salt.
This is my thought: the porter knows my face.
He will let us in, but then you two
will enter boldly to the festal room
while I hold back. Work them up, vex them,
bestir them, drive them from their ease, let nothing
in them not be worried, and then, when all
seems run to ruin, then I'll come and bring
a joyful balm for all their irritations.
I can trust you to trouble them aright?

RABELAIS

No duty is more natural to me.

FRIAR

(to DEATH)

And you, sweet Jester, need do nothing more
than your own droll desire—your strange humor,

protested by your motley robes, will pique
them all to puzzlement!

DEATH

It is my wont
to clarify, but first I must confuse
and throw on everything a vivid shadow.

RABELAIS

There at least she speaks the truth!

FRIAR

How fully does she play the part! Come,
follow close.

(They disappear "behind" the house. The lights come up on the interior. LAVIGNE spins the top absent-mindedly. ALAIN offers MARTINE a drink from his cup. She refuses. He tries to place her crown upon her head and she jerks away. ROBERT studies the fire. VIOLETTE, who has been staring angrily at MARTINE and ALAIN, stands suddenly and speaks.)

VIOLETTE

Well, isn't this a wicked chance!
Five nights running, we've the clearest
skies a heart could wish and now,
at the very hour of our fun,
such a blizzard as never I have seen,
no, nor my mother, nor hers before

beheld such winds and weather bent to wreck
our merrymaking treat!

LAVIGNE

                Come, Mistress Priest,
take heart; the snow can't stop the wine-jug's flow
and that, we know, is why you love your feasts.

VIOLETTE

Watch your forked tongue, my lad—much more
and folk will find another brew to drink,
however sweet your vine! If an honest
girl can't partake upon a holy day . . .

LAVIGNE

Faith then, Father, they've remade the year,
and every day's a holy one, for that's
as often as I serve this sacrament
with you.

VIOLETTE

Hush now! Do you hear him? Shame!

(She swats at LAVIGNE playfully, though looking at ALAIN. LAVIGNE moves aside, otherwise ignoring her, and resumes playing with the top.)

ALAIN

I think the wind is going down.

MARTINE

As ever,
you think only what you hope is true.

ALAIN

Come, I said myself the sky was clearing
as we entered here.

MARTINE

(with disproportionate frustration)
You did, and now
you've dallied here an hour or more until
the snow's blown thick across the ground and you
must walk a mile or more cross-field in drifts.
But for your hopeful thinking you'd be home,
and this unending Christmas would be done!

(Her anger is so unexpected that ALL stop to listen, and no one seems to know what to say. LAVIGNE alone seems unflustered, and as MARTINE, shaking with anger, stops speaking, he spins the top again.)

VIOLETTE

(to MARTINE, speaking mockingly—she is teasing, but there is bitterness behind it)

Now, my girl, the time for that's
both gone and not yet come at all.
Lovers' quarrels are much less sweet
once the betrothal's all complete,

but battle doesn't start aright
till after a brisk nuptial night!

MARTINE
(with despairing coldness)

What would you know of nuptial nights?

VIOLETTE

You little . . .

ROBERT
(he has been paying close attention to this exchange, and speaks at last, interrupting VIOLETTE in a low voice)

Come now, sister, leave her be.
In silence there is charity.

VIOLETTE
(turning on him in anger that seems more than a little tipsy)

Aha! He speaks! And you would break your peace
to fight for *her* against your sister, would you?
A proper little chevalier you are!
We must review your costume! You cannot prance
and posture with these dugs and belly on you!

ROBERT
(standing to take her arm)

I ask you, leave her be.

                    VIOLETTE
            (nearly in tears for some reason)

                    Leave her be!
If only you all would! It'd be her saving,
and each of yours, for her to be let be!

(ALAIN stands aggressively, while ROBERT tries to bring VIOLETTE back to her seat. MARTINE, staring into her cup, does not even turn her head. At this moment, the door slams open, swirling wind and snow into the room, along with RABELAIS and DEATH. Everyone stares. RABELAIS stares back, then advances into the room and addresses DEATH. As he speaks, he arranges the other players in the creche: MARTINE is the Virgin, ALAIN is Joseph, VIOLETTE—holding a cup—and ROBERT two kings, and LAVIGNE is Herod.)

                    RABELAIS

I think we've not yet 'scaped the frigid night,
my dear! Behold: we've stumbled on a scene
so cold its very players have frozen in it!
Transfixed they are, a right tableau, I'd say . . .
perhaps even a creche? Here's the Virgin
and her chaste husband, and here a few Magi—
no, keep your cup, that's your gift!—and this,
plainly, is Herod, contented now to sneer
and wait. See, my own Epiphany!

                     DEATH

There is no child.

RABELAIS

No, the child's here *(indicating himself)* in me! Death
himself, for is not Death a very babe,
the last and littlest of all God's many children?
Here, I nestle against the Virgin's breast—
excuse me—and be-rest myself. How now,
my jesting friend, how strikes you this scene?

ALAIN

(before DEATH can answer)

Get away, you churl!

(He hurls RABELAIS bodily from MARTINE and into DEATH, falling in the process. Both RABELAIS and DEATH stumble, but only RABELAIS falls.)

RABELAIS

(getting up and addressing ALAIN, who remains prone)

Is this how Joseph, king within
the holy home, would greet his guests?
With shouts and kicks and beatings? Even
his foes would expect better treatment
than this absurd display! But we're
no foes, we're only Death and Fun,
come to cheer your eve. *(Addressing DEATH)* Now, Jester,
do your work! Jolly now this feast!

(LAVIGNE and ROBERT rise and approach, herding RABELAIS and DEATH back towards the door, while ALAIN gets to his feet. LAVIGNE hefts a metal candlestick, swinging it easily but menacingly in his hand.)

LAVIGNE

Pardon me, strangers, if I inquire
who you are and how you got in here.
This is no public house or city square,
but the home of one of us, and thus
I'll give you just this solitary chance
to spill your names, your purpose, and your wants
before I escort you back through that door.

RABELAIS

Can't you see? We're Death and his companion,
Laughter! But what's this? Another Death?

LAVIGNE

No, a pilgrim. I've no wit for questings
other than to wander aimlessly.

RABELAIS

Well met, good sir, well met and rare: a man
who knows his limits and explores them well!

LAVIGNE

All well and good, and quite enough;
you've both long outstayed your welcome.
Now get you gone, or risk a ruder
invitation to depart.

ALAIN

Mind, there are two of you, and three
of us, not mentioning that useless
porter—

VIOLETTE
(shouting, clearly fabricating)

He's gone for the marshal,
Alain! They will soon return!

LAVIGNE

Now state your names, that we may know
who has trespassed here, then go.

RABELAIS
(turning to DEATH)

Verily verily I say unto you,
too much kindness for just us two!

(LAVIGNE raises the candlestick while ALAIN and ROBERT move forward. The FRIAR can be seen peeking through the door, but before he can enter, MARTINE darts between the two parties and speaks.)

MARTINE

For shame, Michel! Alain, for shame!
Spurn your best selves if you must,
but leave the rest of us alone
to offer still the God's-own gift

of hospitality! For shame!
Think: if Joseph turned away
in dread or fear on that good night
the Kings, that first Epiphany
would not have been! No gifts, no warning,
and no flight—the very life
of God undone. Come, friends; sit. *(MARTINE takes
   DEATH's arm kindly.)*
This is my home, and these my guests,
and you now too, for I desire
to hear your tale, sing your song;
I could not feast tonight knowing
two souls without were cold and hungry
and I chose not to welcome them.
(To LAVIGNE) Two cups. *(To ALAIN)* Alain, give up your
   seat.

(ALAIN and LAVIGNE seem about to protest, but MARTINE is indomitable. She draws DEATH to sit beside her in ALAIN's seat and indicates for RABELAIS to sit beside DEATH. LAVIGNE, an unpleasant look on his face, takes his own and ALAIN's cups, shakes them into the fireplace, and places them before the two, holding the candlestick all the while and not looking away from DEATH, who seems to have MARTINE fascinated. MARTINE fills the cups with wine from the decanter. ROBERT remains where he was, near MARTINE, and clearly ready for action if necessary. VIOLETTE approaches and hisses in his ear.)

VIOLETTE
(speaking to ROBERT but glaring at ALAIN)

When will he put her down, the cocky bitch?
He ought to leave her to her own conceit—
a quick lashing from that, and my fine lady
would esteem him rightly and too late.

ROBERT

Each love's a law unto itself, and if
it will go down to Hell, it goes clear-eyed,
singing its own tune.

VIOLETTE

                   Oh don't preach.
There's no tragedy surrounding love!
Spurned, I choose to spit; you, to pine.
Your choice is no less odious than mine.

ROBERT

But neither of us chooses not to love.

VIOLETTE

Because we both are paltry fools, and have
not heart nor stomach for the wiser lonely way.
Our flesh is laced too tightly; we can't rip
it off to ease our swollen souls, alas!

(ROBERT seems not to hear her, and as MARTINE begins to speak, VIOLETTE withdraws to her seat.)

MARTINE

Pardon us, noble visitors,
we are not at our best. We had prepared
ourselves for revelry tonight, and masques
and games and sports, at home and in the square,
and comic tales and plays, exotic foods,
and costumes marvelous to see. Never
in memory has this night been otherwise.
No cold, no rain, no frost but amplifies
our joy, elaborates our robes, inflames
us all to wilder games and more fertile jests!
But this year's bitter blight has bested us,
this blast of snow and fire, this icey-faced
inferno unleashed over Earth. No one
dares stir out of doors; no music fills
the streets and squares, and we have learned at last
how frail our merriment is; it is shattered
and can carry us no more. Twelfth Night
is ceded to the sober feastless days,
and for us Epiphany is blind.
But tell us! What brings you here this night
when roads run fierce as torrents and each field
is a battleground? Your robes imply
that you, like us, have failed to join some feast.

RABELAIS

For my part, I went astray—I meant
to break the fast with fellows in Nancy,
but I missed the way, and had I come
not safely here, I cannot say just how
this so misfortuned evening would have ended!

DEATH
(clearly trying to be helpful)

Now that I verily *can* say.

MARTINE
(to RABELAIS)

Apropos your ghastly costume then! *(to DEATH)*
Keep this one close beside you—Death, I mean—
that he might overlook you on the way.
But what of you, my jesting friend? A face
less like to go with motley I've not seen.
What is your game?

DEATH

                      I play no games, lady.
That is my humor: I tell all truth straight,
and that remains always its best disguise.

MARTINE

An honest fool! Truly you are a most
perilous companion!

(She stands, extends a hand, and invites DEATH to dance. Over her shoulder she speaks to RABELAIS.)

Come, Death,
play us a tune. I'll take my chance! I'll dance
your dance, if honest Laughter dance with me.

(She places DEATH in position and steps back, smiling strangely. DEATH's expression does not change. Without turning, MARTINE calls peremptorily to RABELAIS.)

Play us, Death!

(RABELAIS, shrugging, begins to play—badly—a dance tune, something like a canario that involves sharp foot stamps and claps. MARTINE, still smiling, performs her steps perfectly, while DEATH does not move. ALAIN starts to protest, but MARTINE silences him with a look. LAVIGNE looks at DEATH, his face white with terror—it is as if he suddenly realizes who she really is. VIOLETTE puts her hand on ALAIN's arm and speaks to him in a low voice, though he tries to push her away. ROBERT does nothing, but smiles a little as he watches MARTINE.)

RABELAIS
(over his own awful music)

It is borrowed, lady—I really do not play!

VIOLETTE
(angry at being shrugged off by ALAIN, she steps out and dances alone)

Oh come, play on! This din's nicer than silence!

RABELAIS
(scraping away at the music)

At least the ghost of Twelfth Night is not quiet!

VIOLETTE
(still dancing alone)

Ah, this is truly but the ghost of all
our former festivals—our dances round
the fire in the square, the plays, mysterious
and moral, riddles, games, costumes fearful
and frivolous . . . if only you'd have seen it!

RABELAIS
(ceasing to play, and gesturing broadly as he speaks)

But I see it now! Here's the fire,
the dancers, here; in garbs both grand and dire;
what else is needed? With this we all can make
our own feast here, rendering this bleak
night a co-laborer with us
in festival? It keeps us here; it hus-
bands us, creates of us this company
that otherwise would not have been—this body
that else would never have been joined! This night
so grim is author of our tale so bright.

How now, friends? Constrained all round
by wind and rain, how if we astound
this sodden eve and make of it a game?
And not one game alone, but many, tame
and wild alike, a whole deck of games
to tell our fortune, and not only ours
but the whole world's—the fortune, yea, of powers
and thrones, of living things and things struck dumb,
of this life and that of the world to come!

VIOLETTE

(twirls and gestures wildly as she speaks. She seems to be reaching some kind of emotional breaking point)

Games, indeed! Games upon games!
Let us play this wretched night away!

(DEATH, without speaking, brushes past MARTINE, takes the instrument from RABELAIS, and plays. She plays magnificently. RABELAIS takes MARTINE's hand. She waves to LAVIGNE, who reluctantly comes to the floor and bows to VIOLETTE, offering to dance with her, though his eyes stay fixed on DEATH. At this moment, the FRIAR enters, opening the door with a crash. They ALL stop and stare.)

FRIAR

And here's a game to begin!

LAVIGNE

(with the first genuine, decent feeling we've seen from him yet)

Renaud! My friend, can it be you?

FRIAR

Unless I'm changed more than a man should be!

(The two embrace while the others look on, surprised. ALAIN interrupts.)

ALAIN

How are you here? By order of the Order?

FRIAR

(ignores ALAIN and calls to ROBERT)

Robert! Congratulations, sir!
You look as fine as ever I've seen you . . .
I need not ask what you've been doing.

(The FRIAR jerks his hips obscenely, while he and LAVIGNE laugh. ROBERT reddens but does not reply.)

VIOLETTE

What foul wind has blown you here, you jack?

(She embraces him, laughing, then slaps him playfully and steps aside, which leaves the FRIAR facing MARTINE.)

FRIAR

Martine.

MARTINE

Brother Renaud.

(She nods; there is a strong emphasis on the word "Brother." She then steps past him to stand beside ALAIN, looping her arm through his. The pause stretches out and is plainly uncomfortable for ALL except DEATH, who is tuning her instrument. At last the FRIAR speaks.)

FRIAR

And I see you've met my friends,
emissaries gone before me!

LAVIGNE

Met, and rued the chance, and reconciled—
the whole cycle of affection run.

(DEATH plays an experimental flourish on her instrument, and the FRIAR claps his hands.)

FRIAR

And you have drunk, and danced . . . the festival
is underway, I see! Let us go on,
till break of day, and break the night with joy!
Don't let me interrupt the games!
Play on, good clown, and stoke our merry flames!

(The FRIAR sweeps in and deftly catches up MARTINE. ALAIN steps forward in protest, but the FRIAR speaks sharply, pointing at ROBERT in his ungainly costume of a pregnant woman.)

FRIAR

Dance with her—you two are neatly matched!

(He dances with MARTINE well but a little roughly—proprietarily. VIOLETTE laughs wildly and catches up LAVIGNE's hands, drawing him into the dance.)

VIOLETTE

Let's make our shelter from the wild night
wilder even than the storm we fled!

(They dance in these pairs—the FRIAR and MARTINE, and VIOLETTE and LAVIGNE—for a few moments, while RABELAIS and ROBERT clap in time and ALAIN stares angrily at the FRIAR. MARTINE's behavior during the dance is curious: she holds herself stiffly and her face is proud and stern, but at the same time she moves beautifully with the FRIAR's hands. It is clear this is not the first time they have danced together. After a few moments, the music ceases. VIOLETTE falls into a chair, laughing, while LAVIGNE remains standing and MARTINE steps hastily away from the FRIAR and to ALAIN.)

VIOLETTE

Get me a cup, good keep, to keep me moist!
This fire's parching—it dries out all my humors.

(LAVIGNE ignores her, and after a moment she rises and pours herself a large cup of wine.)

FRIAR

Crouched behind that door, I heard whispers
of games. What could be more correct than that,

upon this festal eve? Prick your wits,
I say, each one of you, and drive them up
to frenzy. Propose a game, every one,
in keeping with your nature, and let's play!

(VIOLETTE cheers, RABELAIS smiles, and ROBERT speaks aside gently to MARTINE.)

ROBERT

What do you say?

MARTINE
(who has been sunk in silence since the dance, starts when ROBERT addresses her)

What did you say?

ROBERT

What do you say, Martine? It is your home,
and we all blessed guests in it. Shall we
proceed? Or shall we end this night and leave
you to your peace?

MARTINE
(scoffing)

Peace? What peace is mine?
What night of mine will ever end?
I have no peace, nor festal pleasure
neither.

ROBERT

I would not see your face so sad.

MARTINE

No one compels you look on it.

ROBERT

Are there antics that might bright your eyes?
Speak a word; I will perform them, or attempt.
Or bid me to depart and I will go,
and if you say, I'll rid you of these others,
any here whose presence troubles you.

MARTINE

Unless you are Death himself, and more
than Death—unless you are unbirth itself
and render back to void what once had form,
you cannot rid me of the one who troubles
me, not if you cleared the Earth of all
and left its beauties here for me alone,
for I can view them through my eyes alone,
these fractured crystal windows that distort
and warp the world, and see no world indeed.

ROBERT

A warp is nothing without weft;
alone, no pattern can it hold.

MARTINE
(smiles)

Through all the years that we've been friends, Robert,
I've never heard you say so much together.

ROBERT

I've never had occasion.

MARTINE

So be it. Be my weft, and hold my warp
to shape; so we will weave this tangled night
a pattern yet. *(She briefly grasps his hand, then rises and speaks to the crowd.)*
Games, my friends, we'll have,
and for the first, I do command a play,
and you *(pointing to RABELAIS)* sweet Death, I bid to give us one!

DEATH
(softly but clearly, out of tune with the others' merriment)

But know, midst all your riots and your revels,
Death goes here among you, and by dawn
must make the feast, and eat, and must depart.

RABELAIS
(after an awkward pause, he says patronizingly to DEATH)

Hush hush, my friend—you've muffed your line.
Attend to me, and you'll do fine
next time. *(He turns to MARTINE and bows extravagantly.)*
Had Death a queen, she should be less
lovely than thee, and I less quick
to serve her. Step lively, friends!
You too, Jester! You've no escape.
Show us you can leap and laugh.
A play she wants, a play she'll have,
if I alone must make it so!

ACT II

Scene I: Opens on a "stage" divided in half. ROBERT is seated, still costumed as absurdly pregnant, on a "throne," with DEATH by his side, draped in a white robe or sheet. The FRIAR, dressed as the DEVIL with a beastly mask, a serpentine tail, makeshift horns, and a furry pelt, stands next to LAVIGNE, similarly but less opulently dressed as a MINOR FIEND.

RABELAIS
(theatrically)

Attend, attend, my goodly friends! Attend
to this, our play—a very neat and lively
thing, and suited for a company
like this of mortals and divines commingled!
Marriage of the worlds and intercourse
between: that is our theme. From Heaven
to Earth we'll run our course and back again
till our hard souls do sweat like so much cheese
and down we crash, dead-weary, in the nuptial
bed, and then the real work must begin!
The action opens here in Heaven, where
the Father rules with Wisdom by his side.
To begin, the Devil enters in
and there is speech among them all, to this
effect: beneath the Sun, there dwells a man
not particularly good, or quick,
or sturdy, not too kind or sound or swift,

unremarkable in every way
except for his misfortunes, which are vast.
This man our Devil begs the chance to damn,
which chance the Father's Wisdom sees to grant.
Also, there is a tree.
                    All this shall I,
Providence *(ever laughing)*, unveil
to you, for the joy of crying out
the holy will of God, and for the coy
delight of showing off the Devil's face
confounded, the angel's eyes astounded,
the little ant now crawling, the river-eel
trawling, the morn that dawns, the night that yawns,
the virgin praying in the bed, the wife
obeying in the bed—and husband too!
in the bed and at the board, if all
God's children would go happily . . .

LAVIGNE

Will you shut up and let us start,
that we might quicker play our part
and be set free?

FRIAR

                    Hear hear!
How long will you drag on?
(aside to LAVIGNE) It's best to cut him off early,
for once he's gone, no one can catch him!

RABELAIS

(turning to MARTINE)

What do you say, O Lady fair?
Shall my preface be cut short
to match the manhood of these louts?

MARTINE

(smiling)

We will permit a little more,
and benefit them as they like.

FRIAR

It's a mistake, Martine!

MARTINE

(no longer smiling)

It would not be my first.

RABELAIS

(bows and continues)

Undeterred Providence resumes:
if all God's children will attend to me,
then all God's children will go happily—
for that is the awesome game of God,
that I, Providence, enter laughing: laughing
at the infant squalling in her filth;
at the young ones shitting on the floor;

at the swift strong youth whose every part
serves his will save one! Haha! which wanders
where it wills . . .

LAVIGNE

Like your speech, except
your speech will be cut off. Conclude, or cease!

RABELAIS

All right, all right—so I enter laughing,
for even now the feast is being laid
to mark the troth of God and us, his tetchy
bride! A tickle now, anticipating,
then a kiss, a smack, and all Creation
shall a chorus sing and dance, the players
dance and laugh—yes even she who raged
and he who wept, for it is a wedding
feast! And who can say what babes shall spring
from such a union? So Providence,
in spite of all, laughs, even as
the Devil draggles through the Court of Heaven.

(RABELAIS bows and waves the FRIAR and LAVIGNE onto the stage. LAVIGNE, looking decidedly unenthusiastic, at first refuses, but when RABELAIS begins shaking his fist threateningly, the FRIAR, laughing, drags LAVIGNE onto the stage, where both stop before ROBERT [FATHER, seated] and DEATH [WISDOM, standing]. Everyone is silent, except the giggling FRIAR, until finally DEATH taps ROBERT.)

ROBERT
(gravely)

Oh, it is my line. *(To FRIAR, ROBERT speaks as FATHER)*
So you return.

FRIAR as DEVIL

In one manner, but in another
I never have, and never shall,
and by my nature I never could.

DEATH as WISDOM

What do you implore?

FRIAR as DEVIL

Nothing.

DEATH as WISDOM

Creatures before God may only
praise or beg, never neither.

FRIAR as DEVIL

I come only to observe.

DEATH as WISDOM

So you have come to praise? For in this place
to see is to adore.

FRIAR as DEVIL

Not for these eyes, which merely look
and do not deign to see.

DEATH as WISDOM

What is it that you think you here observe?

FRIAR as DEVIL

I come now from that weary speck
you call the Earth, and there I saw
among the herds of wretched men
one who carried on his tongue
only prayers, and in his heart,
only invocations.

ROBERT as FATHER

I know the man.

FRIAR as DEVIL

As the potter knows the pot
before he flings it to the floor!
This man, as you well know, is doomed
to die in agony, alone,
and not too many days from now!
Even I, to whom the days
to come are dark, can see his fate.

DEATH as WISDOM

He also knows. He has not been deceived.
His sores are let to run, his steps to fail,
his eyes to sag and dim, that he might know
his coming death, and pray, and live always.

FRIAR as DEVIL

Just so! His mind's on you, because
to put it elsewhere were a torment!
You've found, I see, that misery
is just as like to drive a man
to prayer as to blasphemy,
and more are plucked from Hell's fingers
by anguished deathbeds than by quick
demise! But what is the love worth
that seeks God solely from despair?
Take this drab soul that we spoke of:
a fool, poor from birth, unloved,
afflicted now with gaping sores,
sure he's due to die. The only
warmth he's felt came from the rectory
fire, the only mother-touch from stone,
a cold caress from the Virgin's curling hand . . .
it is small wonder he loves you!

ROBERT as FATHER

Why do you care how I shall win my bride?

FRIAR as DEVIL

I say only this: A love
so crudely bought seems less like love
than animal affection. I'd thought
your aspirations higher . . . unless
at last you've learned that things of clay
are only ever muck, no matter
how cunningly they're shaped and wooed.
Give me his care—let me deck him
with riches, and he'll soon forget you!

DEATH as WISDOM

Do you seek to draw us into battle
against you, who are already bested?
Shut your mouth, if only out of pity
for yourself, for even as you speak
your idiocy grows—the only thing
in you that grows. All else in you dwindles,
decays, shrivels, shrinks, while infinite
your idiocy grows. This I think
you think you know, but you've not yet begun
to know the blank bewilderment that shall
encroach endless on you till all
that brilliant intellect from which we wrought
you is obscured, darkened and cut off
forever from its rightful light by ever-
thickening crusts of idiocy, gibbering
alone but for the memory of your past
high faculties, astonished at their loss.

ROBERT as FATHER

Go. Do what you can, for you cannot
do what you will, but do not touch his body.

(RABELAIS/PROVIDENCE enters as the FRIAR/DEVIL crosses from Heaven to Earth. DEATH/WISDOM freezes in place, while ROBERT/FATHER stands, rather clumsily, removes his halo, and crosses to the Earth side of the stage. There he raises his arms, grasping fir branches in either hand, and stands in cruciform, a TREE. VIOLETTE/SUN, still wearing her priest's robes, holds a golden disk. ALAIN/MAN leans against the TREE, and MARTINE/LADY stands slightly "offstage.")

VIOLETTE
(grumbling to herself as she elevates the SUN aloft)

Would I could play the Lady just for once,
instead of dabbling in some minor part!

FRIAR
(overhearing)

No no, you chose the priestly robe—
now you must wear it! Stand and raise
your paper sun. That is your single
task. Up! Raise it now!

VIOLETTE
(viciously)

So she still snares you, you celibate!
Though no one ever thought you
suited for the role, or it for you.

FRIAR

(mockingly)

Bless me, Father, for I have sinned;
forgive my youthful crime of chastity!

VIOLETTE

(jerking her head towards MARTINE)

It's not me who's offended by that crime.

MARTINE

(overhearing)

It's always you offended, no matter what the crime.

VIOLETTE

(snappishly)

What's it to you? The world has me offended,
and no one on its side can be my friend.

FRIAR

Violette contra this shrinking mundi!
I would quake, but *(indicating his DEVIL's costume)* I'm not of
the world—my fate's not bound to it.

VIOLETTE

Ha! There you're wrong, O Prince—this earthly air's
your medium, and when it's gone, so you will be.

ROBERT

Shall we begin, friends?

LAVIGNE

Ho ho, the Tree's limbs tremble! Is the role too taxing for you, man?

RABELAIS

                Begin, begin!
This story has an ending—let us to it!

FRIAR

Oh, now it's not him jabbering,
so we must carry on, must we?

ALL

Begin!

(With a small scuffle, VIOLETTE's SUN rises and ALAIN/MAN, seated beneath ROBERT/TREE, yawns.)

ALAIN as MAN

There's the sun again, and here's
another day, one I'm surprised
to see, yet I'm dismayed, and yet
that copper light upon the field . . .
the mists, the songbirds loose their songs,
this world is not the least of goods!

(He rises, groaning audibly. Behind him, ROBERT's/TREE's limbs quiver—it is clear that his arms are weary, but they do not come down.)

    This fleeting body, how it aches,
    these congealed ashes, yet
    by God's grace, I thirst and hunger, *(he salutes the sun)*
    and go to find what feast I may!

FRIAR as DEVIL

    To throw this puny soul back on his heels
    should be an easy game. I'll hurl him storms
    of splendid things, change his fortune's tune
    to frolic, and blunt his spirit's too-sharp ears.

(FRIAR/DEVIL points, and LAVIGNE/MINOR FIEND whisks out a tunic of rich stuffs, laying it on ALAIN's/MAN's shoulders, then lays a good table. LAVIGNE/MINOR FIEND ushers MARTINE/LADY to ALAIN/MAN, then smites her across the eyes. The scene recommences. MARTINE/LADY approaches ALAIN/MAN and takes him by the arm lovingly.)

MARTINE as LADY

    How came I here? What mystery is this,
    that in the fiercest wilderness I find
    not only vexious dreads and pains but this,
    wondrous vision, intoxicating love!

ALAIN as MAN

    What mystery indeed? This is no place
    for you, Lady—return, please, to your friends.

I will attend you only with this purpose:
to keep you safe, and see you well brought home.

MARTINE as LADY

If not with you, I have no home at all;
send me away, and I go to nothing—
come, where our wedding feast awaits,
with perfumed oil and purest, fresh-pressed linen
to dress your wounds, where in all gentleness
shall maidens robe you, and in all gentleness
shall I, after the feast, unrobe, and all
the anguish of these wounds shall become light
pleasantries beside your greater pleasures.

ALAIN as MAN

What mystery is this? Illusions veiling
all, obscuring . . . do you not see this filthy
flesh? Or am I the one who's blind?
There's some error, but where, I cannot say.

MARTINE as LADY

No error save the primal one of being
made, and that we cannot overcome
save by bathing ourselves in all the unguents
and oils of being made . . . come, you are my mate,
my chosen one, and I would be by you
unmade.

(She takes him by the hand and leads him to the table, where the FRIAR/ DEVIL and LAVIGNE/MINOR FIEND have hastily erected a tent. The two enter.)

FRIAR as DEVIL

And that, my fiend, is how a soul is damned:
she'll succor him, seduce him now with lavish
things, assail his ramparts all about
and leave them shattered, and when his time does come,
it will find him full exposed, and on
his fenceless mind will dawn Hell's darkening day
as once and always it does dawn on us.

(VIOLETTE/SUN begins to set—note that ROBERT/TREE still stands unmoving, though it is in obvious discomfort—and ALAIN/MAN steps from the tent.)

ALAIN as MAN

Some strange blessing's snapped its teeth on me,
an odd and gentle trap, one from which
I dare not seek escape, but Lord, I know
that in full time Thou will spring me from it.

MARTINE as LADY

Husband! Where have you gone? I am alone
and that I will not bear. Attend to me!

VIOLETTE
(in an audible whisper)

Behold how naturally she plays the strumpet!
Her virtue drops from her so clean it seems
That there was never any to begin with!

(ROBERT and ALAIN open their mouths to respond, but the FRIAR interjects.)

FRIAR

We've no time for quarrels, or this play
will never end! Speak your lines, no more,
and save your venoms for another day!

VIOLETTE

When one day those venoms all gush forth,
perhaps you'll wish you'd let them in small drops
and not stopped up the flood until it boiled!

(The FRIAR laughs and gestures ALAIN to continue. Clearly disturbed by VIOLETTE's words, ALAIN returns to his role as MAN somewhat distractedly.)

ALAIN as MAN
(praying)

Give me to bear these goods the same
as Thou did have me bear the bad.

(He re-enters the tent. VIOLETTE's SUN sets. The FRIAR/DEVIL and LAVIGNE/MINOR FIEND exchange looks of dismay and fury. RABELAIS/PROVIDENCE enters. During PROVIDENCE's speech, ROBERT scoots hastily around, replaces his halo, and regains his seat on FATHER's throne.)

RABELAIS as PROVIDENCE

So dismayed, the Devil trails his tail
back to Heaven, where above the Sun
the Father glories in that light unchanging.

(The FRIAR/DEVIL and LAVIGNE/MINOR FIEND return to Heaven, where ROBERT/FATHER sits and DEATH/WISDOM stands.)

DEATH as WISDOM

Return you, then, to Heaven?

FRIAR as DEVIL

Never—it is not in me
to crawl back to the trough I've scorned.
I am no chattel to seek succor
from my exalted torturer.

DEATH as WISDOM

Illumine then your purpose, or depart.

FRIAR as DEVIL

I say this: that you, Great One,
dare not challenge me in open
battle for this peasant's soul.
You give him goods and pleasure, yes,
but then you leave his body anguished;
you allow him dregs of earthly
joy, but forbear from granting
him the simplest thing: pleasure
in his carnal self. And thus
you hope to win your victory
by sleight, and bind him to your love!

DEATH as WISDOM

A curious accusation, and did We
not know you from of old, We would inquire
what slavish liberty you will for him
and whether, for yourself, you've found your leave
from Paradise a good and fruitful one.
What chivalry is this that you imagine
you deserve? The chivalry that tosses
down all weapons and concedes to fight
unarmed a traitor foe, who keeps at hand
a poisoned dagger, close concealed? And yet,
for We cannot be compelled but by
our pleasure, We consent. Heal this human's
frame; perfect his body; make him whole
and wholesome to the eye; straighten his limbs,

brighten his cheek; flush his lip; swell
his limbs with muscle and with fats; shine
his locks with oil; beauty him; grace him
even, with what graces you may steal
from nature—but you may not touch his death.
For he will die, at dusk on the third day,
and as you know, as all now know, you have
no power over death; that is fully Ours.

(Here the FRIAR splutters into laughter and turns to RABELAIS.)

FRIAR

Is it true, O Death? Who orders you
to the tawdry, ticklish things you do?

RABELAIS

Fickl-ish, I think, is better, to describe
those habits life itself can't circumscribe.

DEATH

(cutting in gravely)

Death keeps house at every common crossway;
every movement, every smallest act
is public, yet who directs Death's slightest gesture:
this is of all the gravest mystery.

FRIAR

Our Jester's gone portentous—unpropitious
for our feast, and I suspect malicious.

DEATH

"The Lord will pass over the door of the house, and suffer not the destroyer, the angel of death, to enter."

(ALL are silent for a moment, then RABELAIS laughs.)

RABELAIS

Wrong feast, Jester, you've grabbed the wrong feast!
Loose it, quick, or it will drag us through
the holy year on our behinds, bouncing
right from Christmas into Holy Thursday!

FRIAR

Though if you can contrive a way to speed
us straight through Lent, I won't refuse the ride.

LAVIGNE

Whoever speeds us through this play,
I'll be forever in your debt.

RABELAIS

The play, the play! Our devils bid us play!

(He waves his arms and the players spring into action. While he speaks dramatically as RABELAIS/PROVIDENCE, ROBERT/FATHER edges around and, a little stiffly now, raises his TREE limbs, while VIOLETTE's SUN begins to rise again.)

Armed thus with his God-granted power,
the Devil returns to Earth, bent this time
to fling the Man into his failure through
distractions of the healthful flesh . . .

FRIAR as DEVIL

Must you narrate our every step?

RABELAIS as PROVIDENCE

God save me, no! Only your missteps, sir,
And those are many—indeed, they are Legion.

LAVIGNE as MINOR FIEND

But why? For whom? Who are you talking to?
(Gestures to the "empty" room, the audience.)
Who is this endless entertainment for?

RABELAIS as PROVIDENCE

Why, for life itself! For the very
air, for the rafters, for the hairy
pimple on your chin, for the ether,
for the moon, for the crawling creatures
in our beards, for the pitchéd tents
of snow outside, for the extravagance
that everything is anything at all—
for life, which is the final curtain call!

LAVIGNE as MINOR FIEND

But . . .

ALAIN as MAN

Will you shut up? The more you prick,
the more he'll run, and this dry
game will never yet be done!

LAVIGNE as MINOR FIEND

But . . .

ALL

Shut up!

LAVIGNE as MINOR FIEND

So he may prattle and the rest of us
must hush! This is a tidy tyranny!

ALL

Will you shut up?

(LAVIGNE/MINOR FIEND at last subsides, the FRIAR/DEVIL patting him kindly on the back even as LAVIGNE gestures menacingly with his hands. RABELAIS/PROVIDENCE, grinning, retakes the stage and repeats himself, speaking directly to LAVIGNE/MINOR FIEND.)

RABELAIS as PROVIDENCE

To fling the Man into his failure through
the sweet distractions of the healthful flesh,
the first sign of which is this: The Sun . . .

(He pauses significantly, looking at VIOLETTE/SUN, who is examining her hands.)

RABELAIS as PROVIDENCE

The Sun . . .

(Glares at VIOLETTE/SUN now, who is cleaning under her nails.)

LAVIGNE as MINOR FIEND

Rise, damned Sun!

(He barks so loudly that VIOLETTE/SUN jumps, dropping the disc with a clatter. Blushing, she picks it up and holds the sun straight over her head. RABELAIS/PROVIDENCE gives her a meaningful look as he speaks slowly, enunciating, as if to help her figure it out.)

RABELAIS as PROVIDENCE

The Sun, dawning

(glaring at VIOLETTE until she sheepishly lowers the SUN and begins her prior circuit. RABELAIS/PROVIDENCE smiles and nods)

in her self-same demure
splendor, expecting to discover the Man
awaiting her as was his wont, finds

herself alone. Alone she rises, alone
beholds the pinkish hills and hears the birds;
alone dispels the morning mists and strides
mid the degrees; alone but for thought
of Man within her heart. Meanwhile, within
the tent, Man sleeps, and when he wakes, behold!
no aches, no throb, no stinging in the lining
of the organs, no noxious stabbing round
the joints—nothing, in fact, in flesh to draw
attention but a smack of honest hunger—
which, if you'll permit the note, is by
his night's exertions very well deserved.

ALAIN as MAN

What is this lightness in my limbs? I swear,
one little breeze and I could fly away!

RABELAIS as PROVIDENCE

After his surprise is put away
in herbs, to examine another day,
the Man undoes his hunger swift and neat
with what remains of his cold wedding feast.

ALAIN as MAN

What kind of day is this—a day born old!
*(Looking at the sun, which indicates about eleven in the
   morning.)*

No pains to wake me with the dawn, no cries
to muffle 'neath the morning star, and here's
a feast to make my hunger into pleasure!

(He falls to, and LAVIGNE/MINOR FIEND laughs triumphantly.)

LAVIGNE as MINOR FIEND

No prayer, Master! In abundance
he forgets his lord and shows
already where his loyalty lies:
to you, the keeper of the feast!

FRIAR as DEVIL
(with fury)

Silence! Curse you, gibbet feeder! Crow
this way, your gloating will draw his notice!
Damn this stupid horde I'm forced to lead—
it's little glory to be king of Hell,
when your subjects are fell fools who mock
their foe and little divine his patient ways.
I alone of Hell esteem him right,
I who've pored alone O'er every
moment of his least movement, I,
who hunt him with the patience of a lover,
dissecting all his smallest actions, peeling
back the tissue of his waving hand
to see what bids it stir this way or that;
I study him with cringing care and clutch
at every scattered scrap that he lets fall

behind him on his way and in the darkness
worry it to madness, all in secret. . . .
Alone of all, I have sought to know him
as he knows himself, and for this
I am chastened, I am spurned and startled
out of Heaven and the gates flung shut
around him as around a sacred virgin!
It is for this I am the Prince of Hell,
for I of all things made have dared, pursued,
and been rejected—I alone, you see,
for you and all your ilk did never dare
to dream as high as I, who sought to win.
You thought to grasp, to wrench, to hold and take—
but I to win, and winning, enter in
to trumpet blast and flying flags. I am
a worthy lord. Hell is your rightful realm;
to stay in Heaven would have felt a hell.
You hate Paradise despite its beauty;
I hate it for its beauty, for all the beauty
I could not possess, embrace, become.
Hell is your home, and so you do not feel
its flames as I do, I whose heart aspired
to win Heaven at fair stakes, and sit
down rightly as the bridegroom at the feast.
So you do not know—you fool! Still
you do not know!—that here is the precise
thing he would permit: this lapse, this failure
to give thanks, this negligence of prayer,
that it might lead to greater groveling,

which he calls humbling, before the thought of him.
Silence, then. Do not crow. Not now,
not later, not even when the war seems won
and utterly at end, for that's when all
is poised to be swept up into his hand.

(LAVIGNE/MINOR FIEND, *chastened, says nothing. VIOLETTE's SUN moves across the sky. The voice of MARTINE/LADY calls, and ALAIN/MAN returns to the tent. As the sun is low in the sky, they both come to the table, which the FRIAR/DEVIL and LAVIGNE/MINOR FIEND have reset with fresh dishes.*)

ALAIN as MAN

What fairyland is this? See, wife, here,
awaiting us: good food, and fresh, and wine,
to speed us to our other, better revels!

MARTINE as LADY

Indeed, I see! But call me Lady, please.

ALAIN as MAN

Are you not my wife, my lovely one,
and by this spousing am I not made husband,
of titles known to man but one the fairest?
How could I keep from crying out the beauteous
name, the designation of my life,
the triumph-song, the honorific *wife?*

MARTINE as LADY

All well, all good, I'm sure, but please, refrain
from speaking of me thus. I am a Lady;
I will not be reduced to a wife. *(She turns and re-enters the
 tent.)*

ALAIN as MAN

This coldness puzzles me—she withdraws
when I become most earnest, turns away
when I am eager to annihilate
myself before her. It is mine to charm,
I see, now that I am espoused: first
to win and only then to woo. *(Pauses.)* But how
is this? I have forgotten my own Lord!
In his excess I lose sight of him,
and then asperge my bride for coldness when
at the least flourish of gratuity
my gratitude all vanishes away?

*(He kneels and begins to pray, and as he does so, the sun sets. The two
DEVILS grind their teeth.)*

LAVIGNE as MINOR FIEND

One more day before his death—
one more such and he is lost!
Would that Death were in our power
and we could bid him leave, hang over
this frail man no more that we
might have good scope to work our will!

FRIAR as DEVIL

That must be our theme. Come now, to Heaven
for the final fight: to limit Death!

(The two cross to Heaven, as ROBERT/TREE scuttles around—visible—becoming FATHER again, nearly tripping on his way. VIOLETTE and the FRIAR laugh derisively. ROBERT/FATHER replaces his halo crookedly, and so it remains throughout this scene. ALL assemble in Heaven at last. DEATH alone is totally nonplussed.)

RABELAIS as PROVIDENCE
(suppressing laughter)

So our two fiends flee up to Heaven, where
the goodness sears their eyes and all around
the choir's beauty tears their loathsome ears.

DEATH as WISDOM

Why are you here, back in this land you hate?

FRIAR as DEVIL

Some foul wind returns us to this place.

DEATH as WISDOM

The wind blows where it will. None can resist it.
The wind is the will of God. Why are you here?

FRIAR as DEVIL

I no longer deign to be surprised
by your duplicity, for nothing lies
beyond the limits of your pride, which taketh
even as it giveth just to show
who is indeed the arbiter of all!

ROBERT as FATHER

You come unasked before the Court.
What is your charge, and what your plea?

FRIAR as DEVIL

I come to charge you—yes, You,
who calls himself all Virtue—with this:
the vice of cowardice! It's not
a thing we know in Hell, for we
alone risked all, defied all
and overthrew, if not Heaven,
at least Heaven's complacency,
for we have shown that Paradise
is pusillanimous, the towers
of the Most High timid-built!
Fear bedecks the halls of Heaven,
and spiritless the angels sing,
for they have seen their Lord refuse
the honest struggle and instead

per*fect* chicanery, employ
the holy hosts in subterfuge
and skulk in ploys and artifice!

DEATH as WISDOM

Speak your meaning, if you have not lost
the lovely power of straightforward language.

FRIAR as DEVIL

Oh, how unusually bold of you
to deign to ask what someone else means!
Well, I mean this: that you, who rumbles on
about *love* and touts your so-called *sacrifice*
won't dare assign your best beloved creatures
even a modicum of real freedom!
Ever your downfall, this—for you learned it,
didn't you, from me! You who say
you are omniscient! From me you had to learn
the bitter truth: not everything you make
will adore you, not if you make it free!
I was your first creation, the most thorough,
most like to you; I was intellect
most clear, to best perceive your radiance,
mind most quick to plan and shape and dream,
and will—oh, I was will of fire, will
of iron, will like sharpened burning iron,
piercing as the lonesome stars, a will
the like of which you never dared again!

Will I was, matched to power and insight—
ah, what might we not have done together,
had you the nerve to see me as an equal!
But no. You would be solitaire. And so
you overthrew me, and never again risked
the splendid blend of power and perception
that I am, for you had learned at last
what man has yet to learn: the thing made,
if made greatly, will outpace the maker.
The father always marvels at his son's
achievements. But your arts must not outrun you;
you must hobble them, bind them to bodies
and to birthing and to pain, and if
all else fails, if through magnificence
they defy your limitations, rise
to something great, you fling them down with brute
strength and hand them to your henchman, Death.

(After a pause, in which the FRIAR/DEVIL stands panting with the exertion of his speech, DEATH/WISDOM replies.)

DEATH as WISDOM
(a new gentleness in her voice)

But you forget: there is a Son already.

(She ceases, and there is a long silence in which DEATH/WISDOM is evidently supposed to speak on, but she does not. Instead she stands silently, looking innocently around, as though there is clearly nothing else to say.

Under her breath, she is singing like a child does. At last, RABELAIS/ PROVIDENCE clears his throat and coughs, catching DEATH's attention. She speaks again, unflustered.)

DEATH as WISDOM

And you forget: there is a chosen Bride,
for whom God has been greatly humbled,
for whom has been remade—or soon will be,
it is the same—both Earth and Heaven.
These things you know; this indeed you have learned.
But you, first-made, would not thrive in your sphere.
You would be Son and Father both at once—
you would be Groom and Bride together, lover
and beloved, and dam the course of life.

FRIAR as DEVIL
(to ROBERT/FATHER in a rage)

Will you not speak?

ROBERT as FATHER

In eternity I spoke a Word.
That Word now speaks eternally speaks for me.

DEATH as WISDOM
(to FRIAR/DEVIL)

What is your desire?

> FRIAR as DEVIL
> *(grumpily)*

What I desire you dare not grant.

> DEATH as WISDOM

Answer us or go.

> FRIAR as DEVIL
> *(bursting out peevishly)*

It isn't fair! Who can forget you,
when death hangs over him always?
Send away your servile Death—
let this man live and live and live—
and see if he does not forget you!

> DEATH as WISDOM

Live forever in his flesh?

> FRIAR as DEVIL

Till the end of time, let's say.

> DEATH as WISDOM

That would be to curse our well-loved one.

LAVIGNE

(with an outburst of impatience, throwing down his costume)

I am done with this nonsense. Play on
if you wish, but this game's lost its zest.

RABELAIS

No, no, we're almost through!
Let's see how things will end for them!

LAVIGNE

Play it out yourself. I'm done. *(Pours himself a glass of wine and drinks it quickly.)*

VIOLETTE

(gesturing at him with the sun)

At least you've lines to speak! Come, finish it.
Only a coward leaves so near the climax! *(She winks at MARTINE, who ignores her.)*

LAVIGNE

(raises his glass)

To cowards, then: the wisest of us all!

MARTINE

Come, Michel—play a moment more,
then we'll all drink with you.

LAVIGNE

I won't be wooed. It's now the Pilgrim's turn,
and I've an easy game that all can play! *(Smacks the wine-butt.)*

FRIAR
(to RABELAIS)

He's reached his end. We would do best to drink
with him and let our play burn down to coals.

(ALL begin taking off their costumes with various gestures of impatience or relief, but ROBERT breaks in.)

ROBERT

How does it end?

FRIAR

The Tree speaks! The Father ends his silence!

ROBERT

I'd like to know. How does it end?

MARTINE
(kindly)

The play, you mean?

ROBERT

The man. Does he perish? Or is he damned?

LAVIGNE

Who cares? It's only Alain. Here, wet your throat. *(Hands a glass of wine to ALAIN and points to ROBERT, indicating that ALAIN should deliver it. ALAIN does so.)*

ROBERT

I like to see a tale to its end.

LAVIGNE

Here's where it ends: the bottom of a glass,
and common sense bids us begin again
with something new. Drink up and join us there!

FRIAR

Perhaps you're right, Michel—perhaps it's time
to turn our eyes elsewhere. What game is next?

(He seems relieved to leave the play. He looks around expectantly, but no one replies. VIOLETTE giggles, which may be because she has been drinking quickly and eagerly, and nudges ALAIN in the side. He smiles but shakes his head. He moves to put his arm around MARTINE, but she slips away from him and goes up to ROBERT, smiling.)

MARTINE

Have you a game, friend?

ROBERT

Such things, I fear, are beyond me.
I cannot play the world, nor turn
it to my will; I merely take it.

MARTINE

But that is a subtle game indeed,
and one I think few here could play and win.

VIOLETTE
(turning to ALAIN and shaking him)

Come, Alain, you must have something for us!
You are, after all, our goodly king,
and does a king not owe his people play?

ALAIN
(rises, reluctantly but portentously)

Well, I suppose I could . . .
I could propose a game of riddles.

RABELAIS

The only thing more festive than a play!
What say we all? Shall we game at guessing?

(ALL mumble, nod, shout agreement according to their character.)

RABELAIS

Then we'll begin! And since you *(turning to LAVIGNE)*
did to death our latest game,
it's you must bring to life our new!
Revive us with your keenest riddle.

LAVIGNE

(after thinking for a moment, in which it seems he may refuse, offers this riddle)

I fill the hollow of a tree;
I am the crack within a knee;
I can't but glut an empty gut;
I am the stuffing of a rut.
I swiftly heal a broken heart,
and make of love a simple art.
I do not bear life's ruining scars.
I am the music of the stars.
Who am I?

(ALL are quiet, thinking.)

RABELAIS

I have it! Air!

LAVIGNE

"I swiftly heal a broken heart . . ."

RABELAIS

Ah, yes. *(Goes back to thinking)*

MARTINE
(hesitantly)

Is it . . . It's not death, is it?

LAVIGNE

It's not death, no, though you're near.

ALAIN
(hesitantly, thinking)

Is it…?

LAVIGNE

Yes?

ALAIN
(shakes his head)

Oh, nothing.

LAVIGNE
(bowing)

The king takes it.

ALAIN

What? What did I say?

LAVIGNE

Nothing. That is the answer. Nothing at all.

(ALL smile, repeating lines and laughing at the fitness of the answer.)

RABELAIS

Well offered, wanderer, and well answered, king!
Will you now turn your tongue to wit for us?

ALAIN

(clears his throat)

Here's a little thing of little worth,
but since it is the best I know, I offer:

(With evident pride, he recites doggedly)

    One summer's night, a pair are yoked
    and they their work begin
    and with all joyful things invoked,
    my crop they seek to win.
    The larger one more strongly pulls,
    the smaller steps the quicker
    and by these true and constant souls,
    my field is ploughed together.
    Who am I?

(ALAIN stops and smiles. He is clearly pleased with his effort. MARTINE, however, is not.)

MARTINE
Well, it shambles like an ill-shod horse
if that is any clue. I've no idea.

VIOLETTE
(smacking her half-playfully)
For shame, it is a sweet and pretty thing!

MARTINE
I can't conceive of what it means.

VIOLETTE
(grumbling an aside, but loud enough for the rest to hear)
With a heart as cold as yours, I'll chance
that's not the only thing you won't conceive.

FRIAR
(hastily cutting in)
Any other guesses but Martine's
of shambling steeds? None? Perhaps we might
enjoy the good king's rhymes once more?

LAVIGNE
Oh lords of misrule, save us that at least.

VIOLETTE
(swiftly)

There's no need. I know the answer.

RABELAIS

And?

VIOLETTE

It is sweet matrimony!

ALAIN

Indeed it is! *(Looks tenderly at MARTINE, who ignores him.)*

FRIAR

Well guessed. I never would have caught so sweet
and plump a hare in such a rocky soil!

(VIOLETTE opens her mouth to respond, but RABELAIS intervenes.)

RABELAIS
(cutting off a quarrel)

Fair Violette, your guess is true; the game
has turned to you. Take us behind a name
and show us some thing's nature without shame!

LAVIGNE

This will be rare—bloody, even, I hazard.

(VIOLETTE smiles rakishly at him, then recites, with exaggerated sensuality but never becoming entirely inappropriate, the following riddle.)

VIOLETTE

Each spring my blood rises, thrusting strong
shafts from furred roughness, dense and long.
All of me is good to taste, from stiff
base up my strong heights, good to grip all
swollen as I am with sticky milks. . . .
Oh taste me now, in spring, before I wilt
and fail, my nectars sour and turn sterile!
seize me now, enjoy my splendor, pile
me with kisses, be the summer sun
to draw up all my strength, take me, run
your fingers O'er my brightening tip, breathe
upon my sweetness till I burst with seed!
Who am I?

ALAIN
(with genuine anger)

Such filth! And in my bride's own hearing!

LAVIGNE
(wryly)

She's better off warned, at least.

FRIAR

Hear hear! No one should come to death naïve,
even if it's just a little death!

DEATH
(cutting in)

They only call it so who have not died.

FRIAR

The little vestal spills how much she knows! *(Nudging MARTINE)*
Best take this young droll as your advisor;
keep her close and heed her every word!

MARTINE
(obviously embarrassed, not by the riddle but by the discussion, she speaks scathingly)

I thank you for your kind attentions, but
I think I have no need from such as you,
whose only knowledge of such things must be
either academic or illicit,
neither of which will be my married life.

ALAIN
(turning on VIOLETTE)

I knew you were a flippant, but that you dare
to bring such rhymes before us all—a shame!

VIOLETTE
(stung)

Oh, so *you* go about ploughing fields
and sowing crops but *my* most innocent

lines make you draw back? I promise you,
of us, you're the grosser one by far!

MARTINE
*(to VIOLETTE, trying to be kind, and clearly frustrated with ALAIN
for making a scene)*

I'm not offended by your rhyme,
though I cannot guess its meaning.

FRIAR

It's a darling thing, most suited for
our game. Let's see, let me propose an answer . . .

ALAIN

I forbid you speak what's on your mind!

MARTINE
(with dangerous softness)

Forbid, now, that is a robust word
to bandy in my home.

ALAIN
(taken aback but not standing down)

And yet I won't stand by and permit him—
of all people!—speak obscenities!

MARTINE

Why of all him?

(ALAIN says nothing. The FRIAR breaks in recklessly.)

FRIAR

Yes, why of all me?

ROBERT

This is no time or place . . . *(steps between ALAIN and the FRIAR)*

VIOLETTE
(wildly)

It seems the only time,
the only place, that we shall ever
have this deadening poison drawn!

RABELAIS
(stepping in)

Come, confess to me—Death at least
can be trusted to silence! And perhaps
a good chat will soothe your itchy soul.
(He takes ALAIN gently by the arm.)

FRIAR
(declining to make peace)

He'd best confess to me, for I'm in Orders
and can offer custom absolution!

(ALAIN looks ready to spring on the FRIAR and beat him to a pulp when DEATH quietly breaks in.)

DEATH

I know it.

(ALL stop and turn.)

FRIAR

Know what?

DEATH

The riddle. I know what it is.

FRIAR

Oh ho, she knows it! Spit it out, then.

DEATH

It's dandelions.

(ALL are quiet for a moment except VIOLETTE, realization dawning.)

VIOLETTE

Yes, you darling! *(Hugs DEATH, who is quite shocked by it)*

RABELAIS

Oh well guessed! I knew you'd make
a goodly guest! The stage is yours,
and rightly earned. Riddle us well,
and make our guts with laughter swell!

DEATH

I do not often rhyme and riddle, though
some think me a riddle in myself,
but here's my best. May you find it good.
Dark-sunk stinking hollow, I am a yawn-
ing absence flanked by flaking marble columns
yellowed now. They once were clean and white,
as I once was. Now I am a blight
on all around me, filling now and then
with fetid wind, stinking as a fen,
swamped by fouling streams. I swallow all,
devour and remind that all must fall.
Who am I?

VIOLETTE

A dour tale that, if I may say.

RABELAIS

Not so frolicsome as yours, lady,
but we must give our Jester some license,
she is so newly come into this role.

ROBERT

It is well-wrought, this rhyme.
Is it of your own making?

DEATH

Yes.

ROBERT

There is a music to it,
however grim the sense.

FRIAR

All well and fine, but what's the answer?

MARTINE

Is it the grave?

DEATH

No, though it breathes an air as rank.

VIOLETTE

A tombstone? *(DEATH shakes her head.)* A deathbed?

FRIAR

No double-guessing, especially when
you've just had a turn to speak!

VIOLETTE

What's your guess, then?

FRIAR

I am a blight
Son all around me, filling now and then
with fetid wind, stinking as a fen,

swamped by fouling streams . . . it seems to me
a dung hole fits the meaning passing neatly.

(DEATH smiles and shakes her head.)

RABELAIS

Well, you've bested us! We salute
your wit and promise that the chancy honors
of the next joke fall to you, to do with
as you please! Manifest your meaning!

DEATH
(turning to the FRIAR)

Your guess, good sir, comes the nearest,
though you've gone to the wrong end.
The answer is: that missing tooth
third in your upper jaw, just there.

FRIAR
(stares at her open-mouthed, then lets out a shout of laughter)

By Jove and Bacchus and all that is unholy,
the girl's got me there and earned at last
the right to wear that cap! Do you recall *(nudging ALAIN)*
who knocked out that tooth for me, that one
St. Michael's Day? *(to DEATH)* A butt I'll gladly be
for such a joke as that, my pretty lass!

RABELAIS

And so the grave laughs! Would that I
could fill my duties as ably as you! *(He bows to DEATH.)*

DEATH

Would that it would so laugh forever.

VIOLETTE

Well, you've another chance—no one guessed yours,
so you've the right to pose another or
else pass the chance along to one of us.

DEATH

*(rising, and suddenly seeming by the effect of lights to be much taller and
darker than before, so that the others draw back a little)*

I would I could, but my time runs short,
squandered all in festival with you.
I must resume my work—oh soon, so very
soon! But for the pleasures of this night,
I offer you a gift. I must, by all
God's ordinances, take this night a single
soul of you. But still I have some small
discretion, scant as it may be, and now
I use it to propose to you one final
game to close this Eve of Epiphany.
I come for one among you—now you choose
Whom it shall be, and leave the rest unscathed.
This is my gift, my crowning game, the last

riddle which only one of you will guess.

(DEATH goes to the door, then pauses and looks back at everyone.)
My game is but a simple one.
once you play it, the evening's done,
and all are free to return home
or go where 'ere you choose to roam.
And though the ending may seem cruel,
in this game, there's just one rule:
Whoever next does leave this room
will go forth to his own doom,
and though my clothes say otherwise,
I am ranked high among God's spies,
for I am Death, and Death is I:
follow me, and you shall die.

(She exits the room. The others look around, astonished. Curtain for Act II.)

ACT III

Scene I: Opens with everyone in the same position as at the end of Act II. The scene picks up exactly where the last scene left off, as ALL express confusion and dismay.

LAVIGNE

What trickery is this? Does she try to frighten us?

FRIAR
(turning to RABELAIS)

A strange friend you have there, François.

RABELAIS

I? I never saw the girl till you
walked out of that playful storm together!

FRIAR

But no! I came upon you two
deep in discourse as old companions!

RABELAIS

The devil take me if I ever saw
her face before that very blasted moment!

MARTINE

So neither of you know her, though through you
she came among us. Who is she? Does no one know?

ALAIN

(bristling at the FRIAR)

This is some fresh knavery
even for you, to bring a stranger
into Martine's very home!

FRIAR

This is not my fault!

ALAIN

Nothing ever is though, is it?

ROBERT

(steps between them)

Friends. A strange mistake is on us here,
and we'll not better it by blows. Better,
I think, to ask ourselves: who is this girl?
What is her role, her place? And why this threat?

LAVIGNE

A bold idea, to break in here and glut
herself on food and drink and when the fun's
wound down, to go her way . . . I envy her.

VIOLETTE

A shabby livelihood to skim from place
to place and chew the fat from others' roasts!

MARTINE

I saw her neither eat nor drink. Did you?

(She speaks to ROBERT, but ALAIN answers.)

ALAIN

I swear I saw her raise a glass or two!

ROBERT
(ignoring him)

No. She took nothing.

LAVIGNE

Now you mention it, she did not.
Drink at least, that is.

VIOLETTE
(sneering)

You would track every drop.

ALAIN

It matters nothing who she is! Such obscure
threats won't rule O'er me—if none of you
will dare, I'll go alone and prove the lie!

(Attempts to stride out of the room, but when just one leg has passed the threshold, VIOLETTE catches his arm.)

VIOLETTE

No, Alain! Consider!

(ALAIN wrenches his arm away and stumbles into a table or crock and falls. He receives a deep wound in the leg that passed the threshold. Blood quickly flows, and VIOLETTE screams.)

VIOLETTE

It's true, it's Death! Death is come upon us!

(VIOLETTE dissolves into tipsy hysterics, while ROBERT and MARTINE rush to ALAIN. RABELAIS thrusts them ALL aside and speaks sternly, a new note of command in his voice.)

RABELAIS

Let me! I am a physician! *(Kneeling, he examines the wound.)*
   Rags,
I need rags, and water—hot!—and wine.

(RABELAIS works busily as the stage darkens.)

Scene II: Opens on ALAIN lying on a chaise, his leg bandaged. VIOLETTE sits beside him; she has clearly been crying. MARTINE is on the other side of the room, tipping a bowl of bloody water out of an open window—the wind howls through, and she shuts it. RABELAIS dries his hands on a blood-stained rag and sighs. ROBERT stands with his hand on VIOLETTE's shoulder. LAVIGNE sits, his face in his hands.

LAVIGNE

It was the very part of him that passed
the frame that got the grievous wound. I tell you,
there is evil here, and witchery.

RABELAIS

Well, I've nowhere to be so urgently
as to chance an accident like that,
and though I don't believe in all the things
our pilgrim friend declares are coming true,
if our little Jester proves to be
a hellish guest, surely no harm could come
from lingering here indoors until the cock
should crow and shatter every devil's power . . .
no screech-owl I know of will linger
past that call! *(He claps ALAIN on the shoulder.)* Our patient's
    out of peril.
In the absconding of our clown, it falls
to Death to play our Fool! Follow me,
and I shall bring you, if not rest, some mirth!

> Shall we not beguile the night away
> with one last game, till dawn brings us permission
> to depart and go our ways in peace?

(No one replies for a long moment, then LAVIGNE speaks, barely raising his head.)

LAVIGNE

> All games are futile, and all dawns, and feast-days
> too . . . we see what dawn becomes! That is
> the truest secret of Epiphany,
> the one I witnessed coiled at the heart
> of that strange play . . . we speak of God and Death
> as foes and say we know which one will win;
> we drape his dwelling-place with cloth of gold,
> but turn him round, show us his back, and lo,
> just like the ancient Janus, see our god,
> he wears two faces, and the one behind,
> the hidden one, is Death! They are the same!
> We say that God has conquered Death; we mean
> he has consumed it, and so it has become
> a part of him. The last to be destroyed
> is Death, yes, but only at the end
> of all, when all things else have been consumed
> and there is nothing left for God to do
> but face himself, and then consume himself
> and make an end to Death by ending all!

(He covers his face again and weeps, shocking them ALL.)

FRIAR
(clumsily trying to console his friend)

There, there, it's not so bad as that.
Your picture of a self-consuming God—
oh, very nice and all, but most unlikely.
The world's no awesome tale, my friend. Rather,
it is jumbled chatter in a bar,
punctuated by a tale or two,
sad and splendid tales, sure, but made up
mostly of the disconnected ramblings
of an ever-shifting crowd: a cough,
a laugh, and beneath the senseless muttering
hangs the endless silence that is life.

VIOLETTE

You don't mean that—neither of you!
Life's a cunning maid and odd,
sharp-like and innocent at once,
with no great schemes or lofty aches
but this: to spawn delight, to merry-
make! Don't muddle life with *after*.
It's like mixing wine with water:
one is dulled and the other sullied!
We are here; that mystery
is there. Leave it, I say, and come,
for I've a wicked game to play.

MARTINE
(standing up with great frustration)

Enough of games! Enough! I'm done with all
this forced frivolity, this stiff-necked fun.
Life's no game, neither her kind *(points to VIOLETTE)* nor
 yours *(to LAVIGNE)*,
for your elaborate despair's as stagey
as her relentless frolics . . . life is worse
than despair. It is dull, merely
and forever dull, a waste of passions
growing grayer every year, and shrinking
till your silly sadness does not fit
and all that's left are paltry dooms. Life's no
game, no tale, no tragedy. It ends
in neither death nor marriage, but in a dreary
lessening drip of days in which we feed
and water these, our stupid bodies, stabling
them and currying them until they drop.

ROBERT
(gently, taking her hand)

There is no total lie in what you say . . .
and yet, on a feast day we should play.

MARTINE

And yet.

(She sighs, and squeezes his hand before releasing it.)

Very well, play your games
while you may, and I will play with you,
since that is the dullness sent to me.

RABELAIS

That's the spirit! Take the bludgeonings
of life in jolly humor, and you'll find
they are simply tickles! *(To VIOLETTE)* What's your game,
merry father? We'll dance to your tune.

VIOLETTE

It is a simple game, and one that we
all know very well. But it comes with
a rule: before we play, we all must swear
our willingness, and none draw back at all,
for it's a game will fail if some refuse
to enter in. Do we all so swear?

FRIAR

An unknown compact, with uncertain stakes!
This is the perfect whip to send my blood
to work and set my every muscle tingling!

LAVIGNE

A mindless acquiescence is the mark
of conscious life, so I will not dissent.

ROBERT

I trust you will not compromise our virtue.

LAVIGNE

There's a futile trust!

RABELAIS

Of course I'll play—no use in being Death
if I cherish fear of the unknown.

MARTINE
(turning to VIOLETTE)

I've said I'll play, and now I won't draw back,
but be you warned that once I draw a hand
I play it to the end, and play to win.

VIOLETTE
(ignoring her and turning to ALAIN)

And you, Alain? Will you consent to play?

ALAIN

I'd rather not.

(The FRIAR makes an audible sound of frustration.)
　　　　　　　　　　　　　　But since I am alone,
I will not spoil the game for all. I'll play,
but under protest, and with many doubts.

VIOLETTE

Don't you doubt me, for I'm a priest of God
and all I do conspires to bring good!
Come now, gather all and take your seats
around Alain—we won't make him move.
The game is called Confession, and it works
like this: I will draw lots and call
on one of you at random. Then you must choose
to either speak aloud a secret or
to let me expose some thing that I know!

ALAIN

I do not like this game.

ROBERT

If our lot is drawn, have we no recourse
to avoid exposure and sore shame?

VIOLETTE

Ah but there's the trick! Confess a secret—
any secret, yours or someone else's—
and my apocalypse is kept at bay!

MARTINE

Preserve ourselves by shaming someone else,
you mean. This game reminds me much of you.

ROBERT

I'm grieved to find these machinations in you, sister.

VIOLETTE

Why? Why grieved, why shocked, when all these others
think all other sordid things of me—
why should this special foolery surprise you?

ALAIN

I do not like this game.

LAVIGNE

How if we all refuse to play?

VIOLETTE

(laughing bitterly)

After you gave your word? I'd see you chance it.
Withdraw if you dare, but I've begun
and sure I won't be stopped by act of any
less than God! This weeping sore is full
and it will burst—it will bear no more.
You either play my game and risk your secrets
to the powers of this night, this eve
of revelations, or in the very name
of Epiphany itself I will
throw off these veils and exhibit all,
all alike, all that festers here

within my blistered breast, every truth
revealed without distinction, without succor!
This night will be a night of oracles—
choose if some or all shall be made known!

LAVIGNE

I've warned you all of this, that you all thought
too little of her wrath, and now we're trapped
here in this pocket hell of our own make,
Death without and fiery Truth within!

FRIAR

Oh come come! This is no festive spirit!
One drunken woman's venom is slight threat,
and I've nothing to fear. I say we play.

MARTINE

Nor have I, but I don't like to humor
this flailing rage and honor it with notice.

ALAIN
(quickly and eagerly, with an air of snatching at a good excuse)

Just so! It's not about who is afraid—
surely not one among us keeps such secrets
that he'd betray his friends to shield them!
But this is ugly; I like it little.

VIOLETTE

Insult me as you will, you can't go back.
You must play now, either with canniness
or under threat. The truth won't be balked.

MARTINE

(to the others)

She will play, so let us play also
and see how we may win and wreck her rancor.

VIOLETTE

(clapping her hands)

There! I've never loved you more, Martine—
shirk not from revelation, but instead
seek how you may baffle it! Here,
I salute you *(she kisses MARTINE on the cheek)* and now let us
   begin!

(She draws from her pocket a handful of little scraps of fabric.)
I'm ready, see? I've these bits of cloth,
one for you each—and me, one for me!
No one is safe tonight! Now, if I may . . .

(She reaches over and takes LAVIGNE's Pilgrim hat and drops the scraps in.)
And now I'll close my eyes and choose! What
could be more fair, more beautiful than this,
for is it not beautiful to throw
ourselves on grace and wait?

(The others ALL sit silent and rigid, obviously nervous. VIOLETTE closes her eyes and dramatically reaches into the hat and withdraws a brown scrap of fabric. She opens her eyes and laughs.)

    Tawny is for you, Renaud, brother
    to a fox! What have you to say?

FRIAR

    Ha! Your fishing line is empty, for I
    spoke the truth. I've nothing to confess.

VIOLETTE

    Then whose sins do you offer for your own?

FRIAR

    None!

(The others, who have ALL been clearly anxious, look surprised and relieved. ALAIN lets out a sharp, nervous laugh.)

ALAIN

    That's the way! See, we won't be bullied
    by your little game! We'll hang together!

FRIAR

    It's not for love of you, Alain, no fear,
    but simple curiosity. Our girl's
    a keen-eyed one, but I suspect she knows
    far, far less than she wants to make us think.

MARTINE

(forgetting herself, she grasps the FRIAR's arm in alarm,
provoking a scowl from ALAIN)

Don't reck her less than what she is, Renaud.
She's clever, and in recent days gone reckless.

FRIAR

(laying his hand over MARTINE's,
who looks surprised and withdraws hers quickly)

Violette was always wont to wield threats
in lieu of weapons. Don't you recall her trailing
after us, her little skirts held up,
screaming "wait!" until we'd got away
so far we couldn't hear her? Then we'd hide
and watch her struggle past, threatening and crying
all the time—you'd have betrayed us then,
but for my hand over your lips . . . there now,
I've betrayed a secret. Am I absolved?

VIOLETTE

(fighting back tears of hurt and rage)

That you could always torment little me
is no secret. You're far from free. I know
you crouched there in the trees, mocking me—
I know what other ways you touched her lips!
You say you have nothing to fear from me.
Well, let us see. Shall I tell of all

those midday trysts, the quiet places where
you'd lure her away—though I think
that none of that's as secret as you think . . . ?

MARTINE
(breaking in and looking pale and sick)

Violette, please! Have mercy!

VIOLETTE
(relentless)

I'd tell of that, except that I must honor
every rule I make, and what's revealed
has to be a true secret, unknown
to all! *(To the FRIAR with fury)* I see that smile! I know you think
yourself quite safe. Well, heed to this: I know
what brings you here upon this feast-day eve,
and why you go so lightly, and to where!

FRIAR
(looking suddenly wary, he tries to maintain his jesting tone)

So know we all: I visit from my Order,
and travel here to see my dearest friends.

VIOLETTE
(triumphantly)

Not quite! A rumor ran before you and
I caught it in my traps. You've no consent

to absent yourself from your friary. You,
my friend, have fled, deserted, left your post,
and not for easy reasons, no! You're here,
but your road won't leave you here, for you
are headed to Toulouse to join the Lutherans
who have wrecked our Mother Church! You
forsook your vows and fled, and staked your soul,
or at least your fortunes, all on schism,
and you have high hopes, for you believe
you're quite a plum for them to pluck from Rome!

(They ALL stare in surprise.)

RABELAIS

Is it true, brother?

FRIAR

(trying to make light of it)

I don't know where she gets her ears tickled,
but Rome and Paris envy her!

RABELAIS

You've left the Order and your vows behind?

FRIAR

Oh don't pretend you haven't too, in mind
if not in action! Look at this wide world!
Who would honestly contend that all's

is truly known by but a few in Rome
who likewise offer up such excesses
in local cults and daily shit out relics
ripe to assuage sins—for a cost?
Have I left the Order? No, say rather,
the Order has left me, or better that
there is no Order, and there is no truth,
there are only lumps of circumstance
in which a man may molder in his life long
or, by stepping boldly, overstride
and leave behind. This only is the choice.

(MARTINE, who has been staring at the FRIAR aghast since his secret was revealed, suddenly crosses the stage and strikes him hard across the face, catching him totally off guard. She raises her hand to strike him again but he catches her wrist and grips it. She struggles to withdraw but he grips harder till she lets out a little cry. Then he releases her with a small backwards push and she stumbles back a step, holding her wrist, still shaking with fury.)

FRIAR
(his voice oddly gentle after the confrontation)

I came to tell you this and more, Martine—
these others do not matter. Only you.
And I admit, I thought I'd cause to hope
a greeting very much unlike this one!

MARTINE
(rubbing her wrist and almost weeping with fury)

Oh did you? And just what did you expect?

Kisses? Flowers? Robes spread at your feet?
A festal dance and all things light and sweet?

FRIAR

I came to take you with me.

(Silence, then ALAIN lets out a shout. MARTINE silences him with a gesture. When she speaks again, her voice is low and dangerous.)

MARTINE

I see it now—another broken vow
would be enough to win my heart, you thought!

FRIAR

I made you no vow.

MARTINE

I loved you!

FRIAR

You gave me no sign.

MARTINE

I gave you no bawdy, is your thrust.
I gave to you my heart, my time, my thoughts,

my very life! I gave to you my word!

FRIAR

What can I say? I am a man. The meaning
of a thing alone won't nourish me.
I crave the carnal signs. I know the world
not with my heart, my mind, my thoughts, but with
my mouth, my hands, my tongue. Those are the signs
that I can read. You gave me none of these.

MARTINE

Never have I felt more kindly toward the Church
than now, for she alone and I have felt
this indignity: by you we have
been wanted, wooed, won, and flung away!

FRIAR

Say what you will—I only know one tongue,
that of the body, and in that lovely language
I declare that you'll away with me.

(He seizes her and kisses her, gently but proprietarily. She pulls away and turns to ALAIN.)

MARTINE

Will you do nothing?

ALAIN

Is it true? Did you love him?

(MARTINE starts to wave her hand dismissively, but ALAIN insists.)
Did you?

MARTINE

I thought I did. It was long ago!

ALAIN

And do you still? Love him—or think you do?

(MARTINE says nothing.)
I hear your answer clearer in your silence
than in any words. I leave you free
to think or not to think, as you will,
love or not to love. Our troth is closed.

MARTINE

Alain, I . . . *(He shakes his head and she falls silent, then turns on VIOLETTE in a fury.)*
So this was your scheme, was it?
To dredge up rotting bones and make them dance
your ragged tune, to shatter all our hopes
for union and wreck chaos upon order!
Well, you have your dance, but listen well,
my girl: no one escapes a rising tide;
a surging flood takes all alike to doom!

(MARTINE returns to her seat, shaking with fury. VIOLETTE, after a pause, laughs recklessly and plunges on.)

VIOLETTE

A pretty start, if I may say, to this,
our wildest game! Who can say what other
secrets linger in the hall, just waiting
to be brought to feast, and what may come!

ROBERT

I beg you, sister, stop this now. Have you
not wrought sufficient agony this night?

VIOLETTE
(aside to him)

Why brother, I thought you'd be pleased by this!
Your lady's free and only slightly muddied
by the loves she had before! What fuller
consummation could you dream? *(Aloud to all)* I fear
no agony, only shadows! Come,
drag all our corpses to the light and look
on them—they are less frightful seen full on!
Who's next, to rapture us this sportive night?

(She plunges her hand into the pilgrim's cap and withdraws a scrap of gray.)
The noble pilgrim! *(Turning to LAVIGNE)* So it is your day!
Show the trinkets you have hidden away!

FRIAR

(obviously still smarting, but trying to show some levity)

Take not my doubtful path of courage, friend—
if she says she knows something, heed her!

LAVIGNE

Oh, I'm no hero. I know very well
the reptile secrets she grips by their tails . . .
I've no wish to see them creeping here
from ear to ear with devil grins. But here's
the cunning of this game: If I betray
another's secret, what will you all think
I strove to hide? Will your belief be worse
than truth, or will your charity conspire
to cloak my crimes in gracious robes? To play
this game is to lose—it is all one.
Myself, I cannot bear the certain shame;
I take the shadowed road and let you choose
what to believe of me.

VIOLETTE

Quit stalling! What do you bring to sell?
Sing, little bird, or keep still and hear my song!

LAVIGNE

(looks around at the assembled group, his face drawn; VIOLETTE waits, and just as she is about to speak out, LAVIGNE shouts.)

Robert! I offer you Robert, your kin,

whom I have heard confess a tender love—
and not a courtly one!—for this Martine
whose hand till now was pledged to young Alain.

ALAIN

Do all conspire to rob me of my bride?

VIOLETTE

Pshaw, Michel, this scarcely counts—I've known
for months, and it's my lust that must be slaked!

LAVIGNE

Months! Ha, this goes back years and years
to when the two were youths, and as we hear
Martine was courted by this friar here!

ROBERT
(clearly deeply embarrassed)

I beg you, sister, stop this now.
Are we not shamed enough? Let my
humility suffice, and cease.

VIOLETTE

How kind of you to intervene on his
behalf who wronged you! Sometimes you are too good
to be conceived. *(turning to LAVIGNE)* See, the one exposed

has pled your case—take your tattered robes
and slink away. You'll not be further stripped.
So these two secrets both revolve around
a single lady-love! I wonder she
consents to linger here with us, her self
so much discussed . . . but yes! Where could she go,
with Death at wait beyond this very door?
Play on, we must, for still the winter's night
drags on, and still the saving rooster sleeps.

(She reaches again into the cap. ALAIN whispers to LAVIGNE.)

ALAIN

Can we not constrain her? Must we endure
this pointless torment all in lurching silence?

LAVIGNE

If any could, it's you, but she's gone mad,
and sanity, even supplied by you,
has but small appeal to her now
she's tasted vengeance. She is a lioness
swarmed by bees and stung at last to rage . . .
I always warned you all she could be so!

ALAIN

And always irked her when you could—none more!

LAVIGNE

Hush, it is perhaps your turn!

VIOLETTE
(drawing a slip of cloth, she smiles)
White. *(Turning to MARTINE)* White for you, lady.
It is at last your day to shine!

MARTINE

Choose another.

VIOLETTE

Alas, I too am bound by every law I make!

MARTINE

I beg you, choose another.

VIOLETTE

I won't. Your secret or another's—speak,
or be still and let the judgment fall.

(MARTINE rises and walks to the door. VIOLETTE laughs.)

VIOLETTE

Oh come, surely no thing that you know
is worth the risk of facing what's out there!

(MARTINE stops. She is shaking with some deep emotion. When she speaks, her voice is quiet and very hard.)

MARTINE

You force me to this. Witness, all of you:
I am compelled, and by what force! I thought
to play this game and win, and now I find
I'd rather lose, except that I may not
descend alone, but must drag down some one
of you with me. *(Turns to VIOLETTE)* You drive me here, where I
have long disdained to go, and now I offer
in my place your own most guarded secret,
which has come to me through ways I will
not show but which I swear are true, and if
compelled I will produce the proof—a thing,
I note, you have not offered with your charges.
This I say, and dare you to refute:
that scarce three years ago, to an estate
not far from here you went at Michelmas,
and by the Holy Candles' Day had borne
a child, a son, who lived three days and died
and there was buried, but before he died
you baptized him and called his name . . .

VIOLETTE

Stop!

(Her face is drawn and white, and she has risen to her feet. She points at MARTINE now and cries aloud.)
Stop, you witch! Speak not his name.
It is sacred! You will not say it!

ROBERT

Sister! Then is this true?

VIOLETTE

Would any mother deny her son? *(She covers her face and weeps.)* Though how
she knows, through what dark means, I cannot dream.

ROBERT

Who . . .

VIOLETTE

Don't ask me! Ask me nothing more!
I thought to draw out poison, not
to swallow it again and die again!

FRIAR

Oh hush, you thought to have revenge! And little
dreamed your shame was blacker than your foes'.
I have no pity for you; drink the cup
you forced on us, and see now how it tastes!

MARTINE

(going to her but not touching her)

Forgive me, Violette. I was compelled.

VIOLETTE

Compelled! And by an empty threat!

MARTINE

What do you mean?

VIOLETTE

I know nothing of you—neither good
nor ill. You are immaculate, unstained
by virtue or by vice—you have no secrets!
How different are we two: there you stand,
involved with all of us but oh so far
above us all . . . are you even flesh?
Are you hands that sweat, eyes that ache,
ears that burn, a tongue that sings and skips,
breasts that throb, hips that swell, feet
that dance and cry out after? Are you womb
and wound and awe and grief? Or are you merely
spirit that can ride these things like steeds
and then dismount and go its chilly way?
I know nothing of you, and can for good
or ill reveal of you less than nothing!

MARTINE

And for this I squandered your secret.
O Violette, forgive me!

VIOLETTE

For which part? For winning him whose heart
alone I crave, or spying out my darkest
days, or for being so exalted

that none of this thick world can cling to you?
If there is a comic ending here
it will be yours—from such a blend of soul
and flesh as mine there can come only grief!
Oh why would a kind God make me this way?

(MARTINE tries to console her, but VIOLETTE flings her away. VIOLETTE doubles over and weeps in a wrenching anguish that shocks the rest of them. ROBERT nudges ALAIN, who is looking very red in the face.)

ROBERT

Comfort her. A word from you will end
what volumes from us all could not begin.

(After a pause, ALAIN hitches himself to his feet and limps to VIOLETTE, touching her gently on the shoulder. She wrenches away. He looks confused for a moment, then his face softens and he cautiously puts his arm around her shoulders. The others ALL conspicuously busy themselves elsewhere.)

ALAIN

Hush now. We are good friends of old.
Hush now, and let this foolish game conclude.

VIOLETTE

(still hysterical)

Oh, *now* you call me friend and bid me hush,
now the secret's sprung its trap and flown

to tear me with its talons—only me!
It is always ever only me!

ALAIN

I know this isn't the first time you've stood
between me and my rightful shame; I've wronged
you, little flower, more than once, but now
if you'll allow me I would wholly right you.

(Startled, VIOLETTE raises her eyes to his. Before she can reply, DEATH reappears in the doorway and speaks softly but insistently.)

DEATH

You all do take too long. I've other deeds
to do this night, and must away ere long.
Has this delay brought joy to you, that it
drags on? See, without the storm is calming—
I give you till the first glimpse through the clouds
of moonlight. Then I will compel your choice.

(She withdraws before they have a chance to speak. LAVIGNE rushes to the door, but she closes it behind her softly, and he slams his palm in fury on the wood.)

LAVIGNE

Hey! Listen! You can't do this, you can't
trap us here! We don't believe you! We'll leave
if we want to! Damn you and your games!

RABELAIS
(in the shocked quiet after this outburst)

I think she's not quite grasped quite how
to play the fool. I can't allow
this to go on . . .

LAVIGNE

Oh save your jokes.
They're no good here. This night has gone accursed
and will not end till one—or all—is dead.

Scene III: The same room. Apparently, time has passed—the fire burns lower and people have changed position. VIOLETTE now sits beside ALAIN on the chaise and they are speaking softly; her face is still tearstained but she is smiling, and he looks more at ease and happier than we have seen him yet. MARTINE has withdrawn to a seat beside the fire, and the FRIAR stands nearby, though they are decidedly not looking at each other. ROBERT stands on the other side of the fire, his eyes on MARTINE. LAVIGNE is hunched at the table, spinning his top again. RABELAIS is looking out the window. ALL are far from the doorway.

RABELAIS
(breaks the silence with a dramatic sigh)
O Death where is thy sting? Well, I'd say
it's here, planted tight in all our tails
so we must stand or sit in equal pain . . .
verily, my friend, I've spent many
a strange night, but none so strange as this!
And passed long hours with many a masked companion
who held fewer secrets than the simplest
one of you *(smacks ROBERT on the rump)* and trailed along
   with many
a rollicking and restive crowd towards fire
or a pillory with lighter heart
and lesser doom than dogs me in this cheery
little room which I'm forbidden to leave!
What's on us all this night? A curse? A fate?
Some fairy rage that slides us out beyond

the ken of man? Are we become a footnote
in the tale of salvation? Why
does this Death hunt us so daintily?
I'd be less troubled had one of you folks
dropped dead an hour past than I am now
by all this pageantry! The Earth's haunted
tonight! The smallest squeaking owl's a shrieking
Lilith on the wastes of time, where we
are all beseiged this night! Are we alive
yet, or has our clever little Death
long since undone us all? Is this Hell's ante-
room, and if we pass that door, what fire
will we find—cleansing or consuming?
or is this endless waiting Death? Do we
but linger here, unsought, unmissed, until
that final trump will sound and free us to
Epiphany made barren by delay?

LAVIGNE

You jest, I see, but it is so—
so it must surely be! We are
already dead! *(Turning to the FRIAR)* Some doom you brought
and loosed on us, and even now
our bodies soften in the dying
warmth of yonder fire . . . why else
would all these horrors heap on us
except this is our judgment day!

FRIAR

Come, such drama! To my knowing, no life's
ending comes with all this fanfare. Death's
a quiet thing, and less than we're persuaded
to expect by life. That's the whole game:
death is nothing, and it does not matter.
It has no bearing here—it simply is,
and we are not, and that's the end of things.

RABELAIS

Ah, but the sweet and simple resurrection!

FRIAR

Oh I have found it neither sweet nor simple.
And do you, physician, still insist
on that obscure doctrine? Have you seen any
indication—ever—of escape
from death for any one of us, of looming
victory for life? I have not.
All I have seen, all I have known, teaches
me this: all life, both this one and the one
to come, is here, and what's beyond is but
oblivion, oblivion, I say,
despite the endless soul, for what's a soul
without a body? What's a wind without
the Earth to move upon, a current with
no water, a ripple moving through the void?

RABELAIS

I could not have said it better: The body's
central and won't be disposed of lightly.
You've discerned the problem that so troubled
God during the season of the Old
Testament: how to save the soul
in spite of that unwilling body? You see
his answer. Have you more to say than that?

ALAIN

*(interrupting, he speaks with a new rigor in his voice;
in the middle of this speech, he squeezes VIOLETTE's hand
and rises from his seat, favoring his hurt leg)*

So we intend to stand around all night
and let that witch destroy us all come moonrise?
Who cares about the body's resurrection
or the final meaning of our deaths
when our death need not come to pass tonight!
We've all been too acquiescent, waiting
for whatever comes to pass—no more!
When next this Death comes in to us, let's seize
and hold her fast and find out all her secrets!

VIOLETTE

(leaping to her feet beside him and supporting him)

Hurray! Let's do *something*, even if
it speeds us to our end, instead of waiting
docile here for what we do not know!

I'll follow you, and grasp this Death's cloak-ends
as firm as you, come what mayhem may!

(ALAIN and VIOLETTE smile at each other—there is clearly some new understanding between them.)

ROBERT

Be wise, sister—some weirdness is afoot.

MARTINE

(to ROBERT, looking at VIOLETTE and ALAIN, who have eyes only for each other)

Pleading wisdom in this case seems fruitless.
Look at them, hell-bent to plunge themselves
into some anguish of their own design.
Stop them now and see: madness will drive them
to some other ledge and bid them leap!

(At this moment, DEATH re-enters the room.)

DEATH

I've forborne as long as I do dare.
It's time. Choose: which of you will follow
me and willing take my lonely road?

ALAIN

None! We defy you! You won't make us
accessories in our own demise. *(Glancing around)*

Who's with me? Let's seize our chance
and wring from Death what truth we may!

(Not waiting for a reply, ALAIN springs at DEATH. She brushes him aside easily and he falls. VIOLETTE, meanwhile, catches her arm and clings tightly. LAVIGNE, moved by the courage of his fellows, cries aloud.)

LAVIGNE

Gladly I'll go toe to toe with Death!

(He lunges at DEATH. The FRIAR, laughing with glee at the chaos, leaps into the melee. By now VIOLETTE has been flung off, but is returning to the struggle. RABELAIS seems torn: he clearly loves the spectacle but is unsure what to do.)

RABELAIS

Hey, my friends, but this is less than sporting:
three grown men, and a woman, up
against a half-sprung girl! Come now, let us
not forget the laws of chivalry!

FRIAR
(cackling gleefully and seizing DEATH's robe)

No chivalry in Death, François!

RABELAIS

Now that—that I can't abide. I'll bear
your obscene jokes, your lewd insinuations,
even your grotesque remarks smearing

the resurrection and the holy nature
of all humors—that I'll take, but this
I cannot stand. Fight on, sweet Death! Your Jester
comes to you!

(RABELAIS wades into the fight and delivers a solid punch to the chin of the FRIAR, who stumbles back and nearly knocks over MARTINE. He positions himself in front of DEATH and is pummeled by LAVIGNE and ALAIN, while VIOLETTE dances about shrieking. ROBERT, meanwhile, picks up the FRIAR and hurls him away from MARTINE back into the struggle, where the FRIAR finds his feet with a roar of delight.)

ROBERT

Stop! Stop! This can't go on!

(No one listens.)

MARTINE

Let them fight—they're desperate for it, and
in time they'll tire of themselves and fall.

ROBERT

Before then, someone will be hurt. There's true
rage in there. See Renaud? Beneath
his grins there's deadly fury, and Alain
would give the world to break a head just now . . .
and that slight young woman's in the midst
of it! I will end this, howe'er I must!

MARTINE

Far be it from me to stand between
a good man and his goodness, and you are
verily the finest man I know.
Do what you must, but do return to me.

(Her voice takes on a strange kindness as she speaks, and is positively warm by the end. ROBERT looks at her with surprise, and she smiles.)
Come, what did you say before? A warp
is nothing without weft, and you and I
may make a pattern of this mad world yet.

(ROBERT smiles, grasps her hand briefly, then shoves into the fight. General mayhem rules briefly, until ALAIN, LAVIGNE, and VIOLETTE fall back, panting, showing ROBERT and RABELAIS arranged between them and DEATH. Everyone is bruised and a bit bloodied except DEATH, who appears entirely undisturbed. Behind her looms the open door, completely black.)

RABELAIS

A good bout, if I may say! Brisk
and warming. Alleluia, glory be,
vive le Roi, amen and all such things!

ROBERT

Friends, stop and think! This is no way
to usher in a feast: with blood and blows!

LAVIGNE

It was not us began it, but that wench
who sprang into our midst and threatened us
with death and danger! She's a witch, I swear!

ALAIN

I won't let my friends be handled so.

FRIAR

(panting and smiling)

Besides, what better way to celebrate
a feast of vision than with the clear sight
that comes of striking and receiving blows—
I swear, I see you all more clearly now,
with eyes all bloodied and half swollen shut,
than ever once I saw you all before,
and love you all most truly for the sight!

VIOLETTE

It is not fury that so clears your eyes!
Look! The storm is gone, and the moon shines!

(ALL turn and see the moon shining brilliantly through the window. Outside, the ground glows with fresh snow, but the wind has entirely gone down. As they stare, a cold draft blows through the room, extinguishing all candles but leaving the fire in the fireplace untouched.)

DEATH

It is as I said: until the first glimpse
of the moon. Here it is. The time
is now. I dare not linger any longer.

(As she speaks, a sudden draft blasts down the chimney, scattering ashes and embers and flames around the room. Furniture and curtains catch fire instantly, and in a moment the room is an inferno.)
Choose! Either one will come with me,
or all within will perish, all alike.

(DEATH slips through the door and disappears into the darkness. There is a mad collective dash to the door, but then ALL pause, agonized, at the doorstep.)

VIOLETTE

But what if she speaks truth? I dare not cross!

MARTINE

We all will die if we stay here!

ALAIN

Perhaps a window!

(He tries to get to a window, but the flames are too fierce. He cries out and falls back to the crowd at the door, slapping his clothing to put out the fire.)

FRIAR

Your confessions game came none too soon,
I see! I only hope those absolutions stick.

(He is trying to jest, but his words bring home to all the plight they're in.)

VIOLETTE
(crying and clinging to ALAIN)

I do not want to die!

MARTINE
(in a tone of wondering surprise)

And now it's here, I find, neither do I.

(At this, ROBERT catches her arm and speaks with great urgency.)

ROBERT

Do you mean that?

MARTINE
(still in a wondering tone)

Yes. After all, I find that I would live.

ROBERT
(taking her face briefly between his hands and looking at her intently)

Then live.

(With those words he leaps through the door and into the darkness. ALL stand for a moment, aghast, then with a cry MARTINE screams his name and pursues him, followed by LAVIGNE, VIOLETTE, ALAIN, the FRIAR, and RABELAIS last of all, who pauses for a moment to look back upon the room in flames, then runs into the dark. SCENE ENDS.)

Scene IV: The little group stands outside the house, which is bright but not yet entirely engulfed in flames. DEATH is there, a little way to stage right, and ROBERT stands between her and the rest of the group. The night is calm and beautifully white with snow, and the stars and moon are brilliant overhead. DEATH's face glows in the mix of fire and starlight.

DEATH
(to ROBERT)
I thought it would be you.

ROBERT
I wish you had been wrong.

DEATH
I'm sorry. I do only what I'm asked.

ROBERT
Would that we all could say as much.

DEATH
(reaching out her hand)
Come. It is time.

MARTINE
(breaks away from the group and throws herself between DEATH and ROBERT)

Robert! Don't go!

ROBERT

I must.

MARTINE

No, please! You must remain with us. With me!

(At these words, the FRIAR looks angry and uncomfortable, but no one pays attention to him.)

ROBERT

I cannot.

MARTINE
(returning to her old bitter tone)

You *will* not!

DEATH

He speaks the truth. He cannot stay. No one who is called to go may stay behind.

ROBERT
(touching MARTINE's cheek)

But you may stay, and live, and that is good.

MARTINE

I don't know how.

ROBERT

You will learn, my love. You will learn
to weave your life to shape. You have the strength.

DEATH

Come. It is time, and past.

ROBERT

Goodbye, Martine.

(MARTINE begins to weep, and VIOLETTE steps forward and takes her arm. ROBERT speaks to VIOLETTE.)
Goodbye, sister! I wish you every joy.

VIOLETTE
(speaks to ROBERT snappishly as before but clearly distraught)

To die for such a pack as this!
You were always such a fool,
seeing goodness where there's none.

ROBERT

It's not for your goodness. It's for you.

(He turns to ALAIN and grasps his hand.)
Be good to her, Alain—be better
than you've been to her before.

(ALAIN does not reply, but meets ROBERT's eyes and grasps his hand, looking more confident and handsomer than he has yet.

ROBERT
(smiling, he turns to the others, who are huddled behind in a group)
Goodbye, friends.

DEATH
(insistently)
Come, we must go!

ROBERT
I'm coming.

(He takes DEATH's left hand, which is stretched towards him.)

DEATH
Don't be afraid.

ROBERT
(a little surprised)
I am not. *(He looks her full in the face, and a realization dawns on his.)* Oh . . . but you are!

DEATH
"The last enemy that shall be destroyed . . ."

(DEATH guides him towards her. At the last moment, she raises her right hand high and the cloak, dark inside, arcs up with it, creating a darkened archway. DEATH seems suddenly taller, darker, and grimmer. ROBERT looks at her, and she nods, and her face is gray and grim. He bends slightly and passes through the arch, at the last second releasing DEATH's hand. DEATH lowers her arm, and he is gone. She seems to shrink and is her small, slight self again. MARTINE begins weeping, while VIOLETTE holds her up.)

MARTINE
(lashing out at DEATH while VIOLETTE holds her back)
Curse you! How dare you take the best of us?

FRIAR
(trying to comfort her but unsure how)
It's what death does—it takes the best of us
and leaves the rest to manage how we may.

VIOLETTE
(shrugging him away)
Leave her alone, Renaud. You've done enough.

FRIAR
It's likely not a bad idea—soon
there will be quite a crowd, and questions, many
questions . . . The storm is passed, the day is near,
It's time for me to carry on my way.

ALAIN
(stepping up and putting his hand around VIOLETTE's shoulders)

Then go. Don't dally here for us.
You never did before.

FRIAR
(tries to smile, then speaks to MARTINE)

Martine, I'd hoped . . .
I came here with a hope . . .

MARTINE

You've had too many of my hopes, Renaud,
and ruined them. I have no more to give.
Seek your new companions. May God grant
that they fulfill you more than Church or I.

LAVIGNE

Look. Torches! The village has seen the flames.

FRIAR

Well! That's my cue. Farewell, my friends,
farewell, this madcap night, and last of all
but most of all *(he turns to DEATH and bows)* farewell to you,
   my maid
of many faces. How, I wonder, shall
I know you when I face you once again?

DEATH

You will not. Your kind never do.

FRIAR

Ha! Then I will not try. Farewell, François,
or do you go with me?

RABELAIS

My path lies another way, my once-time
fellow, once-time friend, my broken rhyme.

(They embrace, clapping each other on the back, and the FRIAR turns to depart.)

FRIAR

And be so kind as to forgive me, friends—
I am a loutish fellow, but alive
to life and all its lures. Such is my way,
and thus I am well suited to this world
of spotted humors, the more brilliant-hued
the more they indicate their sure decay!
I am a true knight on a falsied quest;
spurn me, laugh, but see you pity me.

(He disappears offstage, through a back way.)

ALAIN
(gently to VIOLETTE)

You're freezing, dear.

VIOLETTE

Only grieved. Perhaps a little cold.

ALAIN

Come. Let's get you someplace warm.

(He wraps her in his cloak and leads her away. As they reach the edge of the stage, VIOLETTE turns and runs back to MARTINE.)

VIOLETTE

Martine? Have I . . . have we your blessing?

MARTINE

You've no need of it. You never did.

VIOLETTE

But great desire.

MARTINE

Then take it and make merry sport with it—
I've no longer use nor heart for it.

(VIOLETTE kisses her on the cheek then returns to ALAIN, and the two depart together stage right.)

LAVIGNE

I'll go to meet the torches, and explain
what bits I dare of what's unfolded here . . .
would that my memory would soon disgorge
itself of all I've seen and done this night!

DEATH

If that's what you wish, it will. Take care,
though—all revelations are a gift
for those who take them so, and may become
the very nature of a soul's salvation.

LAVIGNE

Death in life is not the way for me.
Even if I walk through life closed-eyed,
I'd still sooner forget than dare to see.
Martine, if you'll with me, I'll do my best
to take their questions and leave you to grieve.

MARTINE

That's kind, Michel, but I will linger here.

(LAVIGNE nods to her and leaves stage left. MARTINE walks towards the burning house and stands quietly in its shadow before exiting stage left, around the house.)

DEATH

(to RABELAIS)

And you?

RABELAIS

I scarcely know. I am all wonderment
at this strange night. But I must ask, good Death:
who was it that you came to take today?

DEATH

Does it matter? What is done is done.

RABELAIS

It was either Renaud or myself,
surely. Which was it? I must know.

DEATH

We all must be content with not knowing.

RABELAIS

Tell me! I cannot rest until I know!

DEATH
(sighing)

I came to one who longed to see,
who feared the world around was cruel.

I came to one who came to me,
and looked, and found his death a Fool.

RABELAIS

Then for me that man . . . *(he looks off to where ROBERT disappeared)* and that shattered girl . . . *(he looks to where MARTINE disappeared.)*

DEATH

I must depart.

RABELAIS
(suddenly recalling)

Your robe! *(He begins to take it off, but DEATH stops him.)*

DEATH

Keep it. I will take it when
I call for you again one day.

RABELAIS

And you keep mine, that I will know you
when you come upon that day!

DEATH
(laughs with a true laughter)

Happy is the man who knows his Death
before it comes! Farewell. Do not forget:
that on this night you taught your Death to laugh!

(DEATH raises her arm again, creating the arch, and stepping through it, disappears into a dark tunnel that folds up after her, leaving no trace.)

RABELAIS
(after a pause)

Such a strange Twelfth Night I've never spent,
nor any night from Eastertide to Lent,
in company with jesters and with kings,
with pilgrims and with priests and darker things
than ever I'd imagined wander here
between cold Earth and where the ether's clear . . .
oh brindled life! whose colors blend and blur
so close the wisest of us can't discern
the line between the wedding and the death,
what's comedy, what's grief, what's void, what's breath . . .
and tomorrow dawns Epiphany,
the showing forth of God's duplicity,
of how he dresses for his bridal feast
and how he veils the finest with the least.
How strange is this Twelfth Night—this final smack
of Heaven and Earth's first kiss, before the crack
of the world's slap! Sweet Earth, virginal Earth,
cold and coy, to have such fecund mirth
sprung upon you like this without warning,
like midnight dawning suddenly to morning!
Is it any wonder that we twist
away, we shocked coquettes, when the tryst
goes guttural—no more those whispered nothings!

Instead, hands, and tongues, and eyes—singing,
our lover's come, and we are unprepared!
Is this comedy, or are we snared
in tragedy? Does the bride weep with rage?
And do we weep with her, or laugh at stage-
paint grief? Or does she sing with joy, and we
all sing with her, or do we sobbing see
the fatal flaw that soon will end her years?
Do all things end in laughter or in tears?
I do not know. I do not know. And yet . . .

(Here he looks around at the burning house, and at the footsteps in the snow, and at the place where DEATH vanished, and he smiles.)

And yet upon this night Death laughed. Forget
everything in life but that: Death,
upon Epiphany, found mirth. The depth
of that's unknown, the import, and the scope—
but maybe after all there's room for hope
that as Christ, the Laughter of the Father,
took laughter down to death, he made them brothers,
and raising one, he equal raised the other,
so even as he bears to God the marks
of death, he leaves in death the very sparks
of merriment! I do not know. No one
can know till down that slippery way he's gone.
But this I know: that I have looked on Death
and laughed, and when I come to my last breath
I'll greet her there, if not as friend, at least
as fellow stranger at this antic feast,
and when my pardoning priest whispers *amen,*

I'll dare to frolic with her once again!

(He exits, going off a different way than anyone else—perhaps through the audience. SCENE ENDS.)

ACKNOWLEDGEMENTS

Thank you to the many writers, editors, directors, and friends who have expressed interest in the Rabelais trilogy and encouraged me to keep going: Danny Fitzpatrick, Ruth de Palileo, Paul Pastor, Tessa Carman, Betsy McClelland, Anthony Sacramone, and Anna Gát, to name just a few. Special thanks to Max Conaway and Tara Isabella Burton for their particular contributions, and a special acknowledgement to Florence Weinberg *(The Wine and the Will)* and Barbara C. Bowen *(Enter Rabelais, Laughing)* for their perceptive and loving analyses of Rabelais's thought. And thanks to my dear family, with all my love.

ABOUT J. C. SCHARL

J. C. Scharl is a playwright, poet, and critic. Her work has appeared internationally on the BBC and in many journals, including *The New Ohio Review*, *The Hopkins Review*, *First Things*, *The Lamp*, *Religion & Liberty*, and others. She is the author of the poetry collection *Ponds* (Poiema Poetry Series 2024), and the verse play *Sonnez Les Matines* (Wiseblood, 2023).

ABOUT TARA ISABELLA BURTON

Tara Isabella Burton is the author of the novels *Social Creature*, *The World Cannot Give*, and *Here in Avalon*, as well as the nonfiction books *Strange Rites: New Religions for a Godless World* and *Self-Made: Curating Our Image from Da Vinci to the Kardashians*. She is currently working on a history of magic and modernity, to be published by Convergent in 2026. Her fiction and nonfiction have appeared in *The New York Times*, *National Geographic*, *Granta*, *The Washington Post*, *The Wall Street Journal*, and more. Tara received a doctorate in theology from Oxford in 2017. She is a Visiting Research Fellow and Lecturer at the Catholic University of America.

www.ingramcontent.com/pod-product-compliance
Lightning Source LLC
Chambersburg PA
CBHW070142080526
44586CB00015B/1801